Escaping the Rabbit Hole

My Journey Through Depression

Tracey Maxfield

Escaping the Rabbit Hole

What Reviewers Are Saying

This book is a "must read" for anyone wishing to gain insight and empathy for the patient, loved one, friend or family member suffering from depression or PTSD . . .
- Dr. Wayne MacLeod, Family Physician, Nova Scotia

All my colleagues read the book, loved it and [are] amazed at [Tracey's] candor, resilience and humor! Most of all the courage to get through every day, not just surviving but contributing. The rawness with which Tracey recollects nearly two years down the 'rabbit hole' and her attempts to find a way out makes for painful but humorous reading, her conversations with DBS (Death by Suicide) her constant companion in the journey, being one example. Tracey shows the resilience of the human spirit, the need to not only survive, but to thrive, to have lived with purpose and meaning. . .
- Rick Nash, Managing Director, Memorez.org, Australia

A real insight of the day-to-day struggles of her own clinical depression . . . She has gone through a living Hell, and all because of workplace bullying. Her strength and conviction to fight . . . each and every day, to beat the ideation of suicide while continuing to have a positive impact on the world of dementia is amazing. She is amazing. This book is a must read . . .
- Dr. Daniel Nightingale, New York, USA

A captivating personal memoir of a brilliant woman who is a nurse and dementia expert . . . an open and truthful account of her personal journey with depression. Tracey's story will definitely empower and give hope to people living with this ignored and misunderstood illness, especially women . . .
- Dr. Meenakshi Noll, Oregon, USA

This read is not watered down. It is achingly thought provoking! We read her blog posts, her journal entries and see her struggle with depression and battle with DBS . . . Tracey informs all how to escape the rabbit hole with treatment, coping, and support. More importantly, she shows there are help, healing, hope and life after depression.
– Lori Snyder of *Lori's Book Loft*

Escaping the Rabbit Hole is a frank and often piercingly . . . painful journey with debilitating depression. Although caring for countless patients throughout her nursing career, Tracey Maxfield came face to face with the one patient who needed her most: herself! Her story and brutal honesty help blaze a trail for others struggling and lost in their own rabbit holes of depression.
– Peter Rosenberger, syndicated radio host and author of *HOPE FOR THE CAREGIVER.*

Dedication

*This book is dedicated to those
who succumbed to the darkness,
who survived the darkness,
and who are fighting the darkness.*

CONTENTS

Part II: The Roadmap of My Survival

Appendices

Foreword

I have spent dozens of hours listening to Tracey Maxfield. Week after week, month after month, she came into my office, neatly dressed, to sit on my couch, and tell me her story.

And as the story emerged, spoken with her British accent and clever mind, something else emerged as well. Part of the story was familiar, something I had heard literally hundreds of times before as a psychologist. A hard-working employee is singled out by [a superior] for a startling and nasty attack. The employee is shattered, confused, and sobbing. They quiver with anxiety, they cry frequently, and they doubt themselves completely. Workplace bullying is all too common, and the devastating effects are almost completely overlooked and ignored by our society. Excellent employees are emotionally abused by toxic bosses, and the organizational culture that enables them. They are left in so much pain that they simply want to die. They go off work because the depression is too crippling. Shortly thereafter, the insurance company contacts them, and starts nattering about a return to work plan. Which adds to their guilt, and intensifies their depression.

What was unique about Tracey was her relentless effort to overcome her psychological injury. Even though she was in a shocking amount of emotional pain, she never gave up. Ever. She dragged herself out of bed, went on her bike rides, went to Starbucks, put one foot in front of the other. Even if she was weeping. Even if she felt covered in cement. As you will read in this book, Death by Suicide was a frequent visitor. She ignored him, she haggled with him, but she did not give in to him. She fought with the ANTs in her brain, she wrote in her journal, she cried a lot, but she never gave up. She had a level of emotional pain that very few people experience, but she did not simply lie down and let it crush her.

Which is why this book is so important to you. Those who journey to far away and difficult places have a great deal to teach us. The Wright brothers broke and fixed and crashed and fixed their little plane dozens of times before they taught us that we are not prisoners of gravity. Nelson Mandela journeyed deep into the solitude of prison before he could teach us that we are not compelled to hate, but can choose to move into reconciliation.

Tracey has journeyed very deep into emotional pain, far beyond where many people have traveled. She can teach you, and me, and all who are fortunate enough to honor her words, that intense psychological injury can be endured, struggled against, and gradually, slowly, overcome.

Dr. Eric Kuelker, Registered Psychologist

Part I

The Journey Begins

1

December 1, 2016

Introduction

Today is Thursday, December 1, 2016. Wow! Only twenty-four days to Christmas and thirty-one days to a new year. It is also 468 days since I fell down the rabbit hole. Although "fell" isn't quite the correct word; a fall is usually accidental, and in my case, there was no accident.

There is nothing accidental about bullying and harassment; it is a deliberate, malicious and intentional act. Instead of falling, I was pushed over the edge and plummeted headfirst, down into an abyss of darkness, despair, pain and sorrow.

In layman's terms, I had a nervous breakdown or, as medical professionals prefer to say, I experienced "an acute depressive episode." Little did I know, 468 days ago, as I lay at the bottom of the cold, dark abyss I affectionately named *the rabbit hole* (when I realised I was going to be staying there awhile), that my life as I knew it was over.

I was about to embark on the most challenging journey of my life: to escape the rabbit hole!

2

December 7, 2016

The Journey Begins

I wish I could say those first few days in the rabbit hole are a blur. Unfortunately, the memory of that time is forever etched in my brain like a tattoo, and while it may not be as painful and vivid now as it was then; nevertheless, it is always there.

For those who have never experienced depression, it is difficult to understand how it makes a person feel. To say that you feel sad and hopeless and cry a lot doesn't come close. Depression is pain, intense, never-ending acute pain. The kind of pain that rips your heart and soul out, shreds your brain into minute pieces, and makes every bone in your body hurt.

It sounds strange to say that you feel physical pain with depression. It is, after all, a mental health illness; but make no mistake: the pain, while different, is very real. I think the best way to describe it is as if you have bruised every part of your body and then your legs are encased in cement boots and you have to wear cement shoulder pads. Every step hurts, every turn of the neck or lift of your arm hurts. You feel so weighed down that it takes every ounce of strength to get out of bed, to sit on the toilet, to climb the stairs.

Those first few days in the rabbit hole, I spent most of my time crawling; the effort and energy required to move was too painful and too exhausting.

And what of the emotional pain? How can I even begin to describe what that feels like? It feels like your very being, your identity, life, and personhood are being incinerated; the pain is heartwrenching. It is raw, and it is constant:

Tracey, you are pathetic.

You are stupid.

You are worthless.

You are hopeless.

You deserve this.

You are nothing.

No one likes you.

No one wants you.

And on and on . . .

You don't know what to do. You feel there is no hope for you. Your entire life has fallen apart and you cannot even fathom how to make things better and get out of the rabbit hole. All you see is darkness; there is no light, not even a glimmer.

And as you lie there, numb and unable to think clearly, your eyes swollen from crying, your body shattered and exhausted, depression decides to introduce you to one of its closest friends: Death, or, as I liked to call him, DBS (Death by Suicide).

3

December 13, 2016

My First Visit with DBS: Death by Suicide

So, what can I say about the first time DBS came to visit? Well, he arrived, without warning on my third day in the rabbit hole.

It was early evening and it was a Saturday. I was lying on my bed, exhausted from hours of sobbing, gut-wrenching, soul-crushing sobbing; trying to stop the never-ending swirl of harsh, critical words resounding in my head; when he arrived.

It happened so quickly that before I knew it, he had crept under the blanket, nestled his head on my pillow and started to whisper. At first, I tried to ignore his voice, but the harder I tried, the louder he became and soon his words started to soothe me: he could help me put an end to all this pain; he could help me find eternal peace and quiet. His suggestion seemed completely reasonable. Why put myself through all this physical pain and emotional torture for another day? The thought of closing my eyes and falling asleep forever sounded like bliss.

And so, I dragged my cement-laden feet up the stairs and rummaged through the medicine basket. I found a bottle of Tylenol (acetaminophen 500mg), emptied the pills onto the kitchen counter and started counting, 20, 27, 32, 40, 44 pills; that should be enough. I poured a big glass of warm water (I never drink iced water) and stood there, staring at the pills.

Go on, DBS whispered, *take them.*

I picked up the first pill and stood there, staring at the mound of white tablets on the counter. I remember thinking *this is it; just do it,* and then, suddenly, I dropped the pill on the counter, ran downstairs, threw on shorts and a T-shirt, grabbed my purse and keys and ran out of the house.

I had no idea what I was doing or where I was going, but I knew I had to go somewhere before DBS convinced me to go back inside and finish the job! And so, I jumped in my car and drove and ended up at Walmart on Banks Road. For the next hour or so, I just wandered up and down the aisles. I must have looked a sight: hair askew, eyes swollen from crying, walking as if encased in cement and seemingly in a trance. Fortunately, no one really seemed to notice. It was Walmart after all (LOL!).

At around 10pm, I arrived back home; went upstairs; replaced the pills in the container; turned off the lights; and, completely exhausted, crept under the blankets and tried to sleep.

For now, I had won the first round with DBS. Unfortunately, he would be back.

4

December 16, 2016

Surreal

Today, I was driving to the mall, listening to the radio, when the DJ announced that Merriam Webster (you know, the dictionary) has released the word of 2016: SURREAL. When I heard this, I started to laugh, because for the past sixteen months the word *surreal* has been my go-to word whenever I try to explain to others, or try to understand, what happened to me, to my life, to my identity, to my very being.

The word surreal means "something that is freakish, unbelievable, unusual, unreal, very strange, or bizarre." All those words describe my life since August 20, 2015. The events that triggered my acute depressive episode and sent me hurtling down the rabbit hole: surreal. My employer's actions towards me: surreal. WorkSafe BC's response to my complaint: surreal. How some friends responded to my acute depression: surreal. How the union treated me: surreal. How LTD (Long Term Disability) handled my claim: surreal. Yes, if I had more time, I could probably write a blog solely about the word surreal!

Anyway, I digress. So, you are probably wondering what happened after I managed to escape the deadly clutches of my unexpected and uninvited new friend, DBS. Did I stay in bed? Did I go back to Walmart? The answer to both questions is *no!* Seriously, who in their right mind goes to Walmart two days in a row? To be perfectly honest, I don't even remember what I did that Sunday; it is a complete blur. But I do know that on Monday morning I contacted my doctor for help.

For over thirty years, many scientists believed that monoamines (mood-related chemicals), such as serotonin, which helps to relay messages across brain; norepinephrine, which mobilizes the brain and body for action; and dopamine, which regulates movement and emotional responses, helping to take action towards a goal, are decreased during a major depressive episode. When I plunged down the rabbit hole, I was taking the antidepressant Effexor XR, which acts on the chemicals serotonin and norepinephrine. However, despite taking the highest dose possible, it was not helping. So, the decision was made to change to another antidepressant: Cymbalta, which acts on the chemicals serotonin and dopamine.

I was told that it might take four to six weeks for me to feel the effects of this new (very expensive, not covered by extended medical) medication. Fortunately, after two weeks, I started to feel a little better. Not jumping around the room, running a marathon better, but the cement boots felt lighter. I had more energy, started to eat more and, best of all, I felt strong enough to go outside and face the world. And so, for the next four weeks, my life became one of routine, routine, routine: awake at 8am, breakfast, medications, watch news on TV, wash, don cycling gear, head out on bike for a two-hour ride up Crawford Estates, onto East Kelowna, then June Springs Road or the Fab Five winery trail. I would return home, make protein shake, shower, get dressed, grab colouring book and pencils, sit on the deck (if sunny) and colour, colour, colour. At 6 p.m. I would make supper, watch TV, do some more colouring, take medications and was in bed by 8 p.m. On the days I did not ride, this list made up my agenda: grocery shopping, errands and visit with the doctor.

This rigid routine became my new life and it was the only thing that kept me going. If I deviated, I would become anxious and go into panic mode. I needed the rigid routine in order to live. This may sound weird, but without performing this orderly list of tasks I knew I would never get well enough to escape the rabbit hole.

Unfortunately, around week six, I noticed the tearful episodes were increasing, I was not eating or sleeping, and those darn cement boots were becoming heavy again. And so, it was decided to increase the dose of Cymbalta from 30mg to 90mg. I was optimistic; the lowest dose had been very effective in the first few weeks. By increasing the dose, I thought it would help stabilize my depression for a longer period and I could finally say goodbye to the rabbit hole.

Or, so I thought, until six days later when I ended up sitting (under threat of certification) in the ER department of the local hospital waiting to see the on-call psychiatrist.

5

January 3, 2017

How Did I End Up Here?

So, I imagine you are wondering how I ended up in the ER. What on earth happened?

Well, when I started to feel a little better and immersed myself in the routine, I also started to sort through my closets, organise the filing cabinet, etc., in an attempt to keep busy. This task is normal for me, and it is not uncommon for me to clean and purge at least once a year. However, this time I could not stop organising and sorting. I posted items for sale on a popular website; I donated boxes and bags full of clothing, books, Christmas decorations, and household items to various goodwill organizations. I cleaned and purged relentlessly, shredding papers, organising photo albums, going through old school books, childhood memorabilia; you name it. I would review the item and then decide whether to keep it, recycle it, donate, it, sell it or throw it out. I couldn't stop, and after I had donated everything, I would return home and look for more stuff to donate.

Needless to say, when I mentioned this to my physician during my weekly follow-up visit, she became very concerned and, after speaking with the on-call psychiatrist, she told me I had to go to the ER department immediately.

I was absolutely horrified! I could not possibly go to the ER (Emergency Department). But no amount of pleading, crying, or begging would convince her otherwise. She was concerned that my behaviour was a sign that I was suicidal.

I was given three choices: go to the hospital voluntarily, but someone must drive me; go to the hospital by ambulance; or go to the hospital under certification part 1 (ambulance and RCMP escort, the Royal Canadian Mounted Police). I finally convinced my physician to let me drive myself to the hospital and call her upon my arrival. If I did not call within thirty minutes, she told me she would notify the RCMP to come find me!

I cannot even begin to tell you how I felt. I had no suicide plan, yet, here I was sitting in the waiting room of the ER department facing the possibility that I may be deemed at risk of harming myself, being certified and admitted to the psychiatric unit. I was absolutely petrified!

And so, for the next few hours, I just sat and waited and watched the clock. I could not walk or sit outside. I literally could not take one step outside the ER department; otherwise, the RCMP would be notified.

When you are awaiting judgment, two hours is an eternity. I kept checking the clock and finding only five minutes had passed. People would come and go, everyone went about their work, ambulances arrived and left, and the hands on the clock kept ticking: sixty minutes until my fate, forty-five minutes, thirty-three minutes. I kept telling myself it would be okay, I was competent, I was sane; but, just in case I was held for twenty-four hours under certification, I began to formulate a plan. And the clock kept ticking.

By now, the tears had long since dried up, and amid the fear and uncertainty, I also started to feel a little angry. I felt as if I had been stripped of my rights. I was a prisoner and, while I was not shackled or confined to a jail cell, I could see the outside world, but I still could not leave.

I began to understand how other people may have felt upon hearing the word *certification*. In the health care system, I think many of us use the word in a cavalier manner, without really giving thought to the impact of the word. Yes, there are people who require certification because they either put themselves in grave danger or put others at great risk of harm or death. But then there are the rest of us who may be going through a crisis, experiencing an unusual event, or just may not like what the medical professional suggests. Yes, we need help, but we do not require certification, and to hear the word, the threat that you may be held against your will for twenty-four hours, is horrible. It strips you of your rights, your identity, and your place in this world. All I can say is, I will never use the word *certification* in the same way ever again.

At 13:47 the Psychiatrist arrived and I was ushered into one of the mental health holding rooms, complete with a locked door and cameras. After reviewing the paperwork, I told him my story, and fifteen minutes later I was told I could go! No admission, no certification, no hidden suicide plan. I was merely experiencing an adverse reaction to the increased dosage of the antidepressant (if you recall from an earlier post, dopamine helps to motivate you to attain a goal and going from 30mg to 90mg sent the chemicals in my brain into overdrive), and it would resolve in a few more days.

That was it! I had just endured one hundred forty-seven minutes of fear and angst, and in fifteen minutes I was told I am sane and competent; keep taking the medication; follow up with my physician in one week, and have a nice day! I kid you not!

6

January 11, 2017

Life in the Rabbit Hole

After the ER visit, life in the rabbit hole continued. As the psychiatrist correctly stated, the side effects of the antidepressant subsided and my home organization and purging ceased. Despite my doctor's fears that I would be angry with her and never see her again, I resumed my weekly appointments. I have a very good relationship with my doctor. I know she was concerned by my behaviour and she acted in my best interests. She was doing her job and, as a healthcare professional, I completely understand.

I continued my daily routine, I took my medications, but still the depression continued. In an attempt to quell the constant, intense, tortuous, emotional pain and anguish, I started to read anything I could find about acute depression: self-help books, websites, research articles on depression, autobiographies. I highlighted passages, I jotted down inspiring quotes. I wrote in a journal, but still the darkness continued. I felt like a dark fog had enveloped me: heavy, suffocating, impenetrable, exhausting; and as I lay there in the darkness, it would wrap its arms tightly around me, hold me close and permeate every cell in my body.

There was no relief. There was no escaping the rabbit hole. The simplest things overwhelmed me. I could not remember people's names. I'd go to the grocery store and forget what I was supposed to buy. I'd drive to the mall, see all the parked cars and leave. I'd go downstairs and forget what I was supposed to do.

Loud noises bothered me, overly stimulating TV shows and movies bothered me, too many colours and patterns bothered me, too many pages in a book bothered me, too many people bothered me. My broken brain just could not handle it. Here I was, a strong, intelligent, capable person who was excellent at multitasking, who could remember patients' details from ten years ago, who never required lists; and now, I was acting like someone with dementia.

I was scared, very scared.

When you are in the rabbit hole, everything changes. The person you once were disappears, the life you once had is gone, and you have to start all over again. Your life revolves around time and tasks.

At first, you exist minute by minute, and your goal is to just summon enough strength to try to complete the most mundane and simple of tasks: get out of bed, clean teeth, brush hair, eat breakfast. Over time, the minutes become hours and now your new routine is to survive hour to hour.

You see, depression has no calendar; there is no tomorrow or two days from now or next week or next month. It is impossible to think about the future, much less make plans; the sheer enormity of trying to understand what you are dealing with and figuring out how to get better and escape the rabbit hole is so completely overwhelming and incomprehensible, the only way you can make it is by staying in the *here and now*. That is all you can do.

And so, with the days becoming colder and shorter, and Winter peeking around the corner, my hours were spent visiting the gym, the doctor, the massage therapist, the psychologist, and Starbucks, where I drank non-fat Americano mistos, read books about living with depression (*Darkness Visible*, *The Mindful Way Through Depression*, *History of a Suicide*, *Change Your Brain-Change Your Life*) and completed the *National Post* crossword.

Now some may say that sounds idyllic. Some may say that doesn't sound like depression. To those people I say it was what I had to do in order to survive, not live, *survive*. When depression takes hold of you, it does not let you live. To live means that you experience life and you experience all that life offers. With depression, you are only given two choices: give up (death) or keep going (survive). And so, in the words of Elizabeth Taylor,

> *"You just do it. You force yourself to get up. You force yourself to put one foot in front of the other, and God damn it, you refuse to let it get to you. You fight. You cry, you curse, then you go about the business of living. There's no other way."*[1]

Once I made the choice to survive, depression decided to up its game, and from out of the shadows appeared an old friend: DBS. Except this time, he'd come to stay, and in order to survive I now had to engage in the battle of all battles, the battle for my life.

---

[1] www.motivationalquotesabout.com/quotes/you-just-do-it-elizabeth-taylor.aspx

7

January 20, 2017

Significant Dates in Life

I think it quite auspicious that I write this blog post on the day of the inauguration of the 45th President of the United States of America. Friday, January 20, 2017, a day that will go down in history, a day that will change the lives of many people forever.

We all have significant dates in our lives: high school graduation, wedding day, birth of a child, death of a loved one, loss of a beloved pet, divorce; and whether good or bad, happy or sad, those dates change our life path.

I remember many significant dates in my life:
- October 17, 1983, the day I started nurse training;

- June 24, 1987, the day I moved, on my own, to Canada;
- November 26, 2003, the day I received my BSN (Hons) in Nursing;
- October 18, 2012, the day I said goodbye to Tag, one of my beloved dogs;
- August 01, 2013, the day I left my home of 19 years and began life as a single woman;
- August 20, 2015, the day I hurtled, head first down the rabbit hole; and
- December 30, 2015, the day I almost died!

I have been delaying writing this blog all week because I know some of you are finding the content of my blogs quite difficult to read (forewarning: this blog may be quite distressing), and because I too am not looking forward to revisiting that awful day and recounting how I came so very close to ending my life.

However, if I am to explain how I eventually managed to escape the rabbit hole, then I must describe everything that happened to me: the good, the bad, and the ugly! (Which incidentally, is also one of my favorite spaghetti western movies.)

So, let's begin. It had been one hundred thirty-three days since I fell down the rabbit hole. Christmas was over, New Year's Eve was only one day away, and soon the year 2015 would be over and a brand-new year, 2016, would begin. Wednesday, December 30, 2015, was a day much like every other day in the rabbit hole.

After a fitful sleep, my usual sleep cycle of getting up three times during the night, I arose around 8 a.m. and began my daily winter routine: eat breakfast, watch the news, read emails, work out at the gym, eat lunch, go to Starbucks, read newspaper, read a book, complete crossword, go home, and watch TV. On that day, I felt neither happy nor sad; I just existed, almost as if on automatic pilot. I could not think about the next day or the New Year. All that mattered was getting through the day, hour by hour: 8 a.m., 1 p.m., 4 p.m.

At 6 p.m., I am unsure why, but I opened the bottle of champagne that I had purchased to toast the New Year. I remember I was sitting on the sofa watching TV, when I started thinking about everything that had happened to me: the incident with my employer, the ongoing harassment they subjected me to, Work Safe BC's denial of my claim, the challenges trying to get my claim approved by LTD, the lack of support from the lead union representatives, the visit to the ER, and on and on.

The problem with depression is that once you allow one negative thought into your brain, it opens the floodgates and every bad, horrible, sad experience in your life comes to the surface. I have always been a thinker. Unfortunately, as many people have told me, I tend to overanalyze things, and with my depressed and fragile brain, overthinking is never good.

The more I tried to understand and make sense out of what happened, the more tired and overwhelmed I started to feel; and it did not take long for the tears to start flowing and the feelings of hopelessness, lack of self-worth, and 'poor me' thoughts to fill my head. Of course, I'm sure that drinking champagne didn't help either.

Suddenly, in the midst of my despair and despondency, I realised I was not alone. An old friend had returned to visit. His name, if you recall, was DBS (Death by Suicide). This time, there was no need for introductions; he knew what he wanted of me. He held me close in a warm and comforting embrace and whispered in my ear:

It is time.

You know what you must do.

Things will never change.

You are worthless.

You are pathetic.

Your life will be forever spent in the rabbit hole.

And so, with champagne glass in hand, I poured myself another drink, walked to my desk, sat down, and calmly began to write letters, goodbye letters. There were no tears; in fact, I felt absolutely nothing. I was completely numb. After I completed the letters, I checked the contents of the safe (will, bank documents, etc.), locked it (I don't know why) and placed the key on top of the letters.

Despite drinking almost three glasses of champagne, I do not recall feeling drunk; on the contrary, I felt very calm and in control. With DBS, holding my hand, I headed back upstairs, walked out onto the snow-covered deck, leaned over and looked at the stone patio below.

Jump! DBS said.

I remember thinking, if I jumped from the balcony, would I die or just be severely injured? I decided I could not take that chance, and so I walked back inside and sat on the sofa. DBS followed, he sat next to me.

There are other ways, he whispered.

I began to think: What could I do? What would be quick and relatively painless? Yes, I know it sounds horrible and scary and morbid, but to be honest, at that moment, it seemed like the right thing to do.

Slit your wrists, DBS said.

I had razor blades, but ugh, too messy, and it would take too long.

Well, DBS suggested, *how about razor blades and pills and alcohol?*

"Hmmn, no," I said. I don't know why, but for some reason that method did not appeal to me. "Okay, maybe pills and alcohol; that will work. Oh wait!" I said. "There isn't enough Tylenol!" Since the first visit from DBS, I only kept small amounts of medications.

Well, DBS suggested, *what about taking all the prescription medications and champagne? That would work.*

"Ah, but wait," I said. "What if I start to vomit? Um, no, better not do that." A few minutes passed.

I have an idea, said DBS. *How about carbon monoxide poisoning?*

Yes! Now that seemed possible. I could drive my car into the forest, park in some secluded spot, attach the vacuum hose to the exhaust pipe, secure it to the partially open rear window and then I could snuggle on the back seat under a nice warm blanket. Yes, that would work nicely.

"Oh, but wait," I said. "What if the police pull me over? Am I over the limit? They'll see the blanket and the hose, put two and two together and take me to the hospital, where this time I will be admitted under certification and put on suicide watch."

By now I was starting to feel very tired. Who would have thought that planning suicide could be so bloody exhausting? I remember looking at the clock; it was 7:40 p.m. DBS took both my hands and led me into the kitchen. On the kitchen counter stood the champagne bottle. There was approximately one glass left.

> *Do it*, he said. *Do it now. It will hurt for a moment but then it will be all over. Do it! Smash the bottle, just like they do in the movies. Smash it and stick it in your neck.*

And so I grabbed the bottle, I raised it above my head, I heard myself scream, and with one almighty swing I brought it down onto the granite counter.

At 2:50 a.m. I opened my eyes. It was completely dark. I felt groggy, my head hurt, and my throat was parched. I was fully clothed, curled up in the foetal position, lying under the quilt of my bed, the pillows and accent cushions completely undisturbed.

I remember thinking, *What the f&*# happened last night? Why am I still dressed and lying on the other side of the bed, the side I never sleep on?*

I slowly made my way upstairs. The lights and TV were still on, the patio door was slightly ajar, and there in the kitchen sink was an upturned champagne bottle, now drained of its contents, and next to it a chunk of granite from the kitchen counter.

As I stood at the kitchen sink, looking at the bottle, the events of the previous evening came flooding back and I started to shake.

At first I refused to believe I had intended to commit suicide. I ran downstairs and there on my desk were the letters, three of them, and the safe key, just as I had left them. I grabbed the letters and with shaking hands I fed them, one by one, into the shredding machine. I could not stop shaking. I could not believe how close I had come to ending my life.

To this day, I have absolutely no recollection of what happened after I smashed the bottle against the counter, all I can deduce is that when the bottle did not break, I realised what I was going to do, ran downstairs, threw myself under the quilt and curled up into a ball. Naturally, the effects of the champagne quickly took effect and I fell asleep.

Champagne 101: Apparently, champagne bottles are extremely tough and designed to withstand high pressure. Consequently, it is very difficult to break a bottle. For example, to ensure the bottle smashes against the hull when it is used to 'christen' a ship, the bottle is scored with a glasscutter to increase its chances of smashing! Guess that was one class I'm glad I failed!

As for the kitchen counter, I decided not to repair it. I figured the chip in the granite would serve as a good reminder of how bad things became that evening and how I almost died!

"Life is tough, but you are tougher!"
- Anonymous[2]

---

[2] www.positiveoutlookblog.com

8

February 2, 2017

He's Always There

DBS (Death by Suicide) is always there. There is no escape.

It's been a while since my last blog, and the delay has been deliberate for two reasons. First, because I know many of you struggled with the content of the last blog, and second, because despite finally escaping from the rabbit hole in late 2016, I am still not truly free of the depression, and DBS is always there at my side, waiting patiently for any moment of weakness, any emotional upset to occur.

In fact, for the past three days, he has been my constant companion, feeding off my insecurities and sense of hopelessness, bathing in my endless tears. Even as I write this, he is sitting next to me, just waiting, quietly, patiently.

Anyway, enough about DBS. In this blog, he will not be the star of the show! So, I guess you are wondering what happened after that horrible night back in 2015. Well, after going to battle with DBS, I spent the next few days in a daze. Despite winning the battle and being thankful that I did not end my life, the depression did not magically disappear. I did not bounce out of bed, glad to be alive. Instead, I was so completely and utterly mentally exhausted and emotionally drained, that for the next few days, I walked around in a fog. I did not celebrate New Year's Eve. I went to bed at 8 p.m. On New Years Day, I resumed my routine: gym, Starbucks, reading, crosswords. Quite simply, nothing changed; life went on, hour by hour. Every single day I would wake up and prepare for battle, a battle to get through the day, a battle to try to reclaim my life, and while some days were better than others, not a day went by without DBS whispering in my ear.

And so, January 2016 soon became February and then March and April.

I would meet friends from work or bump into casual acquaintances and everyone would look at me and comment on how good I looked, how much weight I had lost, and how nice and relaxing it must be having all this time off work!

And I would smile and nod and say jokingly, "Oh, it's all smoke and mirrors," when all I really wanted to do was scream, *Do you have any idea what happened to me? Do you know what I am going through every single day? Do you know what I must do just to stay alive?*

But of course, I didn't. Most people either did not want to know, or did not understand, and sadly, that is one of the reasons why there is still so much stigma attached to depression, to any mental illness.

For the most part, depression is not visible to the naked eye. Yes, there are some people who appear depressed, with unkempt hair, dirty clothing, profoundly sad affect and flat monotone voice, but there are also those people who are profoundly depressed but to all intents and purposes, appear "normal." They dress nicely, they socialize, they go to work, they volunteer, and they are the life and soul of the party.

That is the problem with depression, there are no obvious physical signs; there are no visible scars, no broken bones, no open wounds. But if you could look inside a person with depression, you would see the intense, excruciating emotional pain they are experiencing. A depressed brain is not blue, as most people would think; it is red, hot, burning red, and black, heavy, dark black, and it buzzes constantly, buzzes negative thoughts, sad thoughts, dark thoughts.

The pain is constant and intense and excruciating. I cannot tell you how many times I wish I could rip my brain out and put it under the shower in an attempt to wash away all the pain and soul-sucking negative thoughts. I think that is why so many people turn to alcohol or drugs, not "to let go and have fun," but to try to quell the constant negative thoughts that run rampant through your head. The only time these thoughts stop is when you are very drowsy (drunk/high) or when you sleep; and with depression, you rarely sleep more than three to four hours at a time. And then, when you awaken in the morning, the first thought that runs through your mind, is "oh no, here we go again, another day to get through!"

It just never stops.

And so, with the arrival of April 2016, my body, my soul, and my head were feeling pretty tired and beat up. Yes, I was continuing to win the daily battles, but it was getting harder and harder; and all the time, my sole companion DBS was there, waiting. I didn't want to die, but I also did not, could not, continue to fight this battle every single day for the rest of my life; and so I decided I had no other option but to make a deal with DBS.

9

February 12, 2017

Parole Temporarily Revoked

Well, since my last post, life has been somewhat challenging, to say the least. I'm sad to report that in the past ten days, I have returned to my rabbit hole, albeit temporarily, I hope. Even though I finally escaped the rabbit hole late last year, I am by no means 100% healed; I continue to face challenges, and the usual ups and downs that life offers. Normally, I can deal with one or two challenges, but when faced with many challenges all at once, I do regress and have to return to the safety and seclusion of the rabbit hole. So, instead of fully escaping the rabbit hole, I feel that I am on parole right now. I may be out, but I'm not pardoned yet! LOL.

I'm sure you must be wondering what happened. Well, it was a number of factors, three of them to be exact, that confronted me all in the space of three days:

1. While at Starbucks, following my winter routine, a now retired work acquaintance recognised me and decided to come over and visit with me. This person had directly contributed to my headfirst plunge down the rabbit hole, and yet, here she was, large as life, laughing and smiling like nothing had ever happened, telling me over and over how good I looked, how lucky I was not to be working in that toxic environment.

Now, if she was adept at interpreting body language, she would have seen the look in my eyes, heard the monotone in my voice, and sensed the "get the hell away from me" vibes.

But instead, she chatted away like we were old friends, even invited me to join her at a dance class and other recreational activities, "now that I had so much free time on my hands."

Meanwhile, I sat there, bolt upright, heart racing, throat getting tighter, and resisting the desperate urge to stand up and scream, "Get the f*ck out of here!"

Now, that event on its own, surprisingly, did not send me down the rabbit hole. I actually laughed about it later; however, the very next day, came event number 2.

2. A phone call from the union representative, wanting to update me about the interviews with the other employees who had also experienced bullying, harassment and unprofessional behaviour from the same person as me. In all, eight people gave statements that revealed a pattern of bullying and threatening behaviours from this person over a four-year period.

"Hooray!" I thought, "Finally this person will be held accountable." The union had reviewed the statements and agreed they had enough information to follow-up, but, wait! "They were so busy and short-staffed and had so much work to do," and had decided "this was not a priority right now!"

I was dumbfounded to say the least. I politely ended the conversation and just sat there, stunned, gobsmacked, in shock.

And just like that, I felt myself being propelled back towards the rabbit hole. I just sat there, my feet dangling over the edge, my tears dripping down into the darkness. My brain was buzzing. What now? Why did this happen?

3. I needed to talk with someone, a friend, someone who knew what had happened, and what I was going through, and so I reached out to a friend. Well, to my astonishment and dismay, this friend, despite receiving my call for help, was just too darn busy getting things organised for a trip out of town, in two days time! And just like that, I felt the weight of the cement shoulder pads and the cement boots pull me down into the rabbit hole.

And so, it was back to the doctor, and a referral to a psychiatrist for consideration of possible ECT (electroconvulsive therapy), plus the addition of another antidepressant to my medication regime.

So here I am. It's Day 8 of the new therapy and I think the fog is starting to lift. DBS is in his rocking chair, patiently waiting, but we have an agreement, and so he backs off, for now. I am sleeping better, my appetite has returned, and I have resumed my bike rides at the gym. I am confident that I will be back out on parole before the week is over. Oh, and before I forget, the person I reached out to is no longer privy to this blog.

10

February 21, 2017

The Deal

So, by now, you must be wondering what deal I made with DBS. Well, the deal was to try to let me live for the next few months and, if by September 9, 2016, I still hadn't found a way out of the rabbit hole, then he could take me!

Yes, I know it sounds horrible and sad, but when the majority of my days were consumed with darkness, sadness and sheer exhaustion from trying so very hard not to surrender to DBS, I felt it was the only sane thing I could do. In fact, it gave me a temporary reprieve, so on the really bad days, instead of fighting DBS, I would say, "Just keep going. Give it a chance. Only a few more months and, if things haven't improved by September 9th, then you can say *goodbye*."

And so, that was my mantra for the next nineteen weeks. Every day I wrote in my journal and recorded the things I was thankful for: a sunny day, a chocolate croissant, a good book, a beautiful flower, a smile from a stranger. To be honest, I felt like I was starting over again and had to look at the world, and at my life, with fresh eyes and a new perspective.

With the arrival of spring and sunny weather, I could forego the gym and resume my outdoor bike rides, and so began a new routine and a new escape plan. I would ride thirty-five kilometers, five days a week, up into the hills, along the lakefront, East Kelowna, past the orchards and wineries. Wherever there were hills and lots of them, I would go ride them.

In the afternoon, I would sit on my deck and read books, lots of books: self-help books, fiction and autobiographies. I coloured books on mandalas. I copied any inspiring quotes and self-help suggestions that resonated in me in a book.

As I became fitter, faster and stronger, I took lessons in SUP (stand-up paddle boarding), outrigger canoeing and surf skiing. You could say I tried to keep myself so busy that I didn't have time to think! Let me tell you, depression and thinking are not good friends!

Did I have bad days? You bet I did! My new life was not easy. I still awoke at 3:30 a.m., and every day, I would force myself to get on my bike and ride. I can't tell you how many times I rode my bike with tears and snot running down my face. I would read and suddenly start crying or feel overwhelmingly sad and despondent. I would shower and sit clutching my legs to my body, the hot water raining down on me, as I sobbed and screamed out for the pain, the endless excruciating pain to go away. But, I had made a deal, and so I would get back up and try to keep moving forward.

In the words of the great leader Winston Churchill,

"If you're going through hell, keep on going."[3]

And so, April became May and then June, and the days started to get better. I set myself some goals: ride my bike up a nearby mountain, SUP (stand-up paddle board), OC1 (one-person outrigger canoe) and surf ski across the lake and back (5.2km).

---

[3] https://www.brainyquote.com/quotes/quotes/w/winstonchu103788html

Unfortunately, life with depression can be misleading, and one of the biggest challenges I had to learn to deal with was this: whenever I had a good day, I had to embrace it and record it for future reference because the very next day, I would wake up back in the rabbit hole, enveloped in the darkness, being weighed down by those cement boots and shoulder pads.

The month of July was difficult. I continued my daily routine, I went out with friends for a glass of wine or dinner, but whatever I did, wherever I went, DBS came with me. I'm thinking he may have been following a different calendar from the Gregorian calendar. LOL!

As I battled against DBS, I decided to track the days to see if there was a specific reason or time of the month that precipitated this sudden decline again. Every day, when I wrote in my journal, I assigned the day a number from 0-10. Similar to a pain scale, it was my personal depression scale, 0 being assigned to DBS and 10 being the most amazing, awesome, incredible day ever! Any number under 5 was not good, as in down the rabbit hole with a vengeance; any number over 5, I considered to be an okay day, with 7 being a good day. (FYI, I still use the scale and I have yet to experience a day higher than 7 because any number higher than 7 means absolutely no visits from DBS.)

As I write this blog, I am looking at my journal and all I see, page after page are the numbers 2, 3, 4, 5:

July 7th - 2

July 10th - 5

July 18th - 4. Tomorrow is another day. I must keep going until September 9th, 2016

July 24th - 4. I am so weak and pathetic!

July 25th – 3. I am completely and utterly exhausted, I feel like I am wearing cement shoulder pads and am just drained of any feeling or emotion, just absolutely done.

July 30th - 3. I just want to be done with everything because the pain is just wearing me out. Day in, day out, and to be perfectly honest, I don't even think it's worth pushing ahead until September. :(

Finally, July draws to a close and a new month begins, August, a time to begin again. Little did I know it was going to be the most difficult and challenging month yet.

11

March 3, 2017

A Glimpse into the Depressed Mind

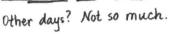

I am so very lost and lonely, standing bereft at the crossroads of my life. And it doesn't matter which way I go; they all lead back to the rabbit hole and eternal darkness and loneliness forevermore.

12

March 5, 2017

DBS, My Stalker, in Plain Sight

August 2016 will go down as one of the most difficult months I experienced since I had fallen down the rabbit hole. Despite the warm sunny weather, going bike riding in the mornings, paddle boarding in the afternoons, and sipping wine on the deck in the evenings, I could not shake the feelings of intense anxiety, sadness, hopelessness and dread. Some days were so dark, so bad, I could not even write in my journal.

On August 9th, I was scheduled to fly to Arizona and spend some time with my girlfriend and family, but as the date came closer and closer, I was filled with panic and dread. I felt so vulnerable and scared and lost, and I feared I would not survive the trip. I existed on two hours of sleep per night, my head constantly buzzed, my heart and soul felt completely empty, and every minute of every day I struggled to find a reason to live, to keep going until September 9th.

Every morning I would tell myself, "Only four weeks till eternal peace. Just keep going. Only four more weeks."

And so, on August 9th, I boarded a plane to Arizona.

Those who know me know that in the past fifteen years or so I have become one of those "grip the armrest really, really tight" type of fliers, and I always carried sublingual Ativan with me, just in case I felt I was going to have a panic attack. Well, guess what! Apparently, when you have depression, there is no panic attack or grabbing the armrest, because you are numb; you don't feel anything.

And so, when we flew into a horrendous sandstorm as we approached Phoenix, and the plane dipped and dove and jumped in the air, I think I was probably one of the calmest on the airplane. Go figure!

Despite my fears, the week in Phoenix, albeit sweltering hot and alcohol-fuelled, was relaxing and nice, and for the first time in months, I started to sleep through the night. Yes, the sadness and heaviness continued, and I cried every single day, but lying by the pool, bathed in sunshine and warmth, I felt strong enough to fend off the advances of DBS and keep going.

On August 17th, I returned to home, and within a few days, I could feel myself relapsing. No matter what I did, he (DBS) was there! I'd ride my bike and think how easy it would be to swerve into one of the big trucks racing down the hill. I'd go paddle boarding on the lake, and think how easy it would be to go out into the middle of the lake and just slip into the water.

And then, THE day I had been dreading arrived: August 20th, the one-year anniversary of my descent into the rabbit hole. One year since my mind completely detached itself from my body, my soul, my life, my everything. One year since I lost all that was important and dear to me. One year since I had worked. One year since happy, fun-loving, confident, capable, organised, intelligent, witty Tracey had disappeared without a trace!

The anniversary awakened so many memories. I felt like I had been catapulted back in time and I could hear those nasty, mean, hurtful, vicious comments; the horrible lies; the false accusations spouting from my bully's mouth. Even as I type this, I can feel my neck and shoulders begin to tighten. It was, and still is, one of the most unbelievable and soul-decimating experiences of my life. It still feels surreal, and I still cannot believe that I made it this far.

Anyway, as you can imagine, the next few days were extremely painful and challenging. Forget the old adage "sticks and stones may break my bones but words will never hurt me." Whoever wrote that was either deaf or a psychopath, because bones heal, but hurtful words imprint themselves on the brain like an acid tattoo! And so, for the next few days I sought refuge in the rabbit hole, desperately trying to stop myself from surrendering to the warm embrace of DBS. I even marked off the days on the calendar until September 9th, in an attempt to hold off his unwelcome advances.

September 9th was a beautiful day: blue sky, sunshine and just a hint of fall. I had not slept the night before because my eye was swollen and very painful (apparently it was a corneal abrasion) and needless to say, I was feeling pretty crappy. As it was decision day, I had to see my doctor to discuss how I was feeling and what my plan was. To be honest, I was so preoccupied with the pain in my eye, I really wasn't thinking about it.

My appointment was scheduled for late morning, and as I drove to the doctor's office, one of the local radio stations announced that today was a very important day for Librans (I am one): "Finally, after twelve years of challenges and misfortune, it's time to celebrate, Librans. Lucky Jupiter has moved into your sign and the year ahead will be filled with good fortune and divine protection!"

Now, I don't believe in horoscopes, but I started to think maybe, just maybe, this was an omen, divine intervention. Call it what you will, but hearing those words actually gave me a small glimpse of hope, and I started to wonder: maybe, just maybe, I could go on a little longer. And so, when I met with my doctor, I told her I was changing the plan.

Sometimes it takes an overwhelming breakdown
to have an undeniable breakthrough.
- Anonymous[4]

---

[4] www.TheDailyQuotes.com

13

March 18, 2017

Adrift in the Ocean and No Land Ahoy

This is a very hard blog for me to write, and consequently, I think it will likely be a very difficult blog for many to read.

This past week has been quite challenging. After experiencing five good days in a row, for absolutely no rhyme or reason, I could feel myself being drawn back to the rabbit hole, and the more I fought, the quicker I fell. Although I did manage to climb out and push myself to keep going, after only a few days I fell hard and fast.

The reason: a chance encounter in the grocery store with a work acquaintance and allowing myself to be drawn back into that dysfunctional, highly toxic world. The meeting spanned a mere five minutes, but it was enough time for the brain cells to reopen and absorb the poison. When poison is poured into a severely fractured, depressed brain, not only does it hurt, but it also stirs up old feelings and emotional distress.

By the time I arrived home, my head was buzzing. This may seem strange, but the only sound I heard was an intense high-pitched buzzing. It was as if there was a multitude of electrical signals firing in the brain at the same time and I could not think clearly. I couldn't hear myself think. It was intense, completely over-whelming, extremely painful, and I felt that I must be going insane.

I have found the only thing that helps is to NOT think, and perform a simple task, like washing the dishes or folding laundry, and eventually the buzzing stops. Unfortunately, once the brain quiets, the exhaustion sets in and the tears flow in gut-wrenching, nose-running, eye-swelling sobbing. And the more I berate myself for not being stronger, for reacting, the weaker and more beaten down I feel until I realize that I may never get better, and this is it: my new life.

It is at this point, when I feel I have no more fight left, no more of me to give, that an old, familiar friend appears: DBS, my constant companion, my stalker in plain sight, my worst nightmare, who also, maybe someday, will be my saviour.

The funny thing is, I do believe the new antidepressant is helping. For me to experience five consecutive days with no tears or bad thoughts or visits from DBS is amazing. On the downside, the bad days are really bad. There is no halfway, no so-so day or average day; it feels like I am being dragged to the edge of the rabbit hole and down I go. There is no soft landing, nothing to grab hold of. I hit hard and fast. And, just like that, I don the cement boots and shoulder pads and prepare for battle, the battle for my life, because You-Know-Who is waiting for me in the shadows.

I guess one positive aspect to living in a rabbit hole is that with medications and therapy and lots and lots and lots of work (I think I could be a therapist I've read so much. LOL!), I am now able to find my way out more quickly. But the sheer effort and energy it takes to fend off DBS and get the hell out of the rabbit hole are starting to take their toll.

Nineteen months of living in the rabbit hole, nineteen months of escaping the rabbit hole only to fall back in, over and over again, and for what? My doctor just completed more paperwork for LTD and described my condition as "serious, very long recovery, ability to work again is extremely guarded." Hearing those words jolted me and scared me. They also made me so very angry! How can a person, an organization, do this to someone, to me?

I have been a nurse for almost thirty-four years. When I was two years old I bandaged my teddy. At eight years old I kept a note-book full of medical terminology, first aid techniques, and different diseases. At nineteen years old, I spent a year working with blind and deaf children, adolescents in care, babies and children with special needs, and adults with dementia. At twenty years old, I entered nurse training.

Nursing is all I have ever done, all I ever wanted to do. Now, to be told that I may never be able to work as a nurse again is devastating. It is heart-wrenching. It is beyond comprehension. I feel that the final chapter has just closed on the book of my life *as it was*. I do not know if there is a new book waiting for me and, if there is, what this book is about. I don't even know what the opening sentence of Chapter 1 is.

And so, here I am, fifty-three years old, sitting on a raft, adrift in an ocean, which is my life, and the sharks are circling, and the seagulls are overhead. In the far, far distance, I can almost make out land; but I have no map to guide me, so I don't know how to get there. The question is: do I let the tide carry me? Or do I pick up the oar and paddle? Or do I slip into the water?

I won't give up without a fight, so today I paddle. But tomorrow and tomorrow and tomorrow? I just don't know.

14

April 2, 2017

Trying to Be Okay
with Not Being Okay All the Time

Well, here I am, still sitting on the raft, adrift in the ocean of my life. Ahead of me I see a faint outline of land and out of the corner of my right eye, I see more land, a little smaller and less distinct, so maybe it is just an island or an atoll.

Since my last post, the new antidepressant appears to be effective, and I am feeling a little better about myself and my "new" life. I have picked up the oar and begun paddling towards the shape in the distance; however, at this time, while it seems I have done a lot of paddling, I don't feel I have gotten any closer to this unknown land mass.

My psychologist tells me I am being too hard on myself, and I have got to learn to take it a day at a time, and so, I am trying a new mantra:

I am trying to be okay with NOT being okay all the time!

What this means is that when I feel myself falling back down the rabbit hole, I do not fight it. I accept that it is happening and trust in myself, my inner strength, my determination, and my spirit that I will be okay, and I will climb back out. So, on those bad days, of which I have had a few, I stop paddling, lie down on the raft, close my eyes, and try to enjoy the warmth of the sun (Oh, did I mention, my ocean is somewhere in the Caribbean? Hey, a girl can dream, can't she? LOL.). Of course, this is easier said than done, because the great white shark, DBS, continues to circle the raft (apparently sharks do not sleep!), hoping that I'll dip my feet in the water and then he can pull me under.

My blog posts have been a little disjointed lately, jumping from the past to the present. Today, now I have given you a brief update of how I am doing, I thought I would continue recounting my escape from the rabbit hole. Believe it or not, I really did escape; however, I continue to lease the space and use it when my parole is temporarily revoked!

So, let's quickly recap. It was September 9, 2016, my final day; but en route to my doctor's appointment, after listening to my horoscope for 2017, I reconsidered my decision. And much to DBS's chagrin, I changed the plan. Needless to say, my doctor and psychologist were relieved, albeit temporarily, because I had already decided on another plan; however, this plan was different. It was clearer, more focused, had a much longer timeline, and gave me a chance to truly escape the rabbit hole.

The month of September was good. The weather was nice, sunny with a blue sky and a hint of fall crispness in the air. I continued to ride my bike, working toward my goal of riding up the mountain. I continued to read different books, working toward my goal of one hundred books read by end of 2016. And I continued to work through my depression and attend therapy.

In October, the weather became much cooler, but I continued to ride; and on Saturday, October 15, despite the grey cold weather, I donned my thermals and rode to the top of the mountain. It took thirty minutes to get to the top and a mere three minutes down, but what a ride! Not only was it an accomplishment, it was invigorating, exhilarating; and as I was fighting through the fatigue and intense muscle pain in my legs, and telling myself to keep going, I had an idea: Maybe I should write about my experience with depression.

By the time I reached the top of the mountain and looked out across the magnificent lake, the grey clouds parted, and a sliver of sunlight peeked through. And just like that, I knew it was the right thing to do.

Unfortunately, I could not put my plan into action for some weeks, as the remainder of October and early November were particularly hard for me. The dark, thick clouds of depression permeated my brain, I developed a nasty cough and cold and before I had a chance to grab my comforter, I was back down the rabbit hole.

Despite making a new, long-term plan, I can always rely on DBS to sidle his way in and start wooing me with comforting words and promises. By November 12, I had to pull out the big guns, and thanks to a kind and supportive friend, I added an SAD lamp[5], or as I like to call it, my 'happy light', to my arsenal of rabbit hole weaponry. Toward the end of November, I was feeling a little better, and despite entreaties from DBS to stay longer, I successfully climbed out of the rabbit hole and began to decorate my Christmas trees and adorn my home with twinkling lights.

On December 1, I finally created my blog, *Escaping the Rabbit Hole: My Journey Through Depression*, and wrote my first post.

---

[5] A SAD lamp is a form of light therapy used for Seasonal Affective Disorder (SAD), a type of depression that occurs in Fall and Winter.

15

April 7, 2017

Swimming with the Sharks

You know, the funny thing about rabbit holes is you can wake up one morning and discover sometime during the night you fell back in, and you have no idea how or why it happened.

After so many good days, some spent paddling, some spent resting, DBS, the great white shark, decided to throw caution to the wind, ditch the new plan, swim really close to the raft, and start pushing me off course.

It was so sudden, so completely unexpected, I could reach out with my fingers and touch his dorsal fin. I tried to reach for the oar, but my limbs were already weighed down with cement. My brain started to crackle and buzz; and as the thick black fog descended, and began to infiltrate every cell in my body, I was overwhelmed with exhaustion.

I had completed so many journeys, so many challenges, and part of me wondered: If I suddenly grab hold of the dorsal fin, will I just ride around on his back, or will he plunge into the depths of the ocean? And if I swim to the surface, will I make it, or will he grab me in his jaws, shake me like a toy and bite me until all that is left is some skin and bones? Did I mention I don't like sharks?

I wonder if any of you have ever felt a shark's skin. It's not smooth; it feels like sandpaper. How do I know? Well, when I was eleven years old, I took a sunset dip in the sea, swam a little too far out when something in the water began to bump and nudge me. I had no idea what was happening to me; I was absolutely terrified. When I finally made it back to shore, my legs were covered with red marks and welts. The following day, the newspaper headlines read: *School of Basking Sharks Seen in the Bay!* Yes, I know they are not predators, but the following year, *Jaws* was released; I have never swum in the ocean since!

But, I digress. So, as I felt myself slowly surrendering to the darkness, I remembered the words "today, it is okay to not be okay" and I realised I had a choice: I could accept that I will continue to have very bad, dark days and I will also have good days, or I could jump into the water and become fish food! Did I mention, I really, really don't like sharks?

And so, on day 594 of fighting this horrible depressive disorder, I decided to give myself a break from fighting and just be present in the moment. Yes, I know it sounds cliché, and it is easier said than done; however, I was willing to try a different approach that will help me to overcome the self-defeating, self-persecuting thoughts that pop up in my brain.

I made a tight fist with one hand and pressed my fingers deep into my palm and told myself "it's okay to not be okay all the time." The pain from my fingernails temporarily distracted me and disrupted the negative thought pattern.

It may sound strange, but right then it appeared to be helping. After what I had been through and will continue to deal with, that's good enough for me.

16

April 16, 2017

The Things People Say

As I've mentioned in earlier posts, my reason for writing this blog is twofold. Firstly, it is a safe place to document my journey through this horrible depression and, secondly, I hope my posts provide some insight and education in the world of depression. I hope one day I will be able to "go public" with this blog; however, if I am ever to achieve this goal, I know I must be emotionally stronger so I can deal with any negative comments, "helpful" advice and criticisms that inevitably occur with public blog posts.

As we all know, the world is full of people with their own thoughts, beliefs, opinions and ideals and, even if they know little or nothing about a specific illness, religion or political issue, this does not stop them from having an opinion.

Sadly, ignorance can be dangerous. It can create fear, hatred and social isolation. It can perpetuate myths and misconceptions. I strongly believe that is why so few people will actually admit to themselves and/or others they have depression. They fear how others will react, what others may say and how they may be perceived in the world.

Very few people know I have depression because I too am very aware of the social stigma, of being thought of as mentally ill or crazy. When people hear the word *depression* they are unsure what to say. They know what depression is, but many are unsure how to respond. They don't want to say the wrong thing. Some people are more comfortable and ask questions or offer support. And then there are people who really should have just kept their mouths closed!

This weekend is Easter, a time for bunny rabbits, spring flowers, family dinners and chocolate eggs, lots and lots of yummy chocolate eggs. It is also a time of great spiritual and religious awakening for so many people.

Therefore, I thought I would take a break from my usual dark and heart-wrenching blog posts. Instead I will share some new research about depression and also share ten of the strangest comments people have said to me upon being told that I have depression.

When you read it the first time, you will probably be aghast. I was, but now I realize that in their ignorance they really did not know any better. Now I can laugh and respond with a quick comeback.

After years of taking a one-size-fits-all approach to depression, many researchers now recognize there are likely many variants of the illness, and each might respond best to a particular treatment. Possible treatment options are:

- Celebrex (anti-inflammatory) can alleviate symptoms for people on antidepressants.[6] Omega-3 fatty acids may also help decrease inflammation and improve mood.[7] Researchers are now working to develop an anti-inflammatory medication that targets depression.[8]
- IV Ketamine (an anesthetic), also called Special K (not the cereal) on the street, reduces symptoms in treatment-resistant depression patients. Unfortunately, there can be uncomfortable side effects, e.g., nausea and an out-of-body sensation. Carlos Zarate, Jr., M.D., Chief of Experimental Therapeutics & Pathophysiology Branch and Section on the Neurobiology and Treatment of Mood

6 http://www.medscape.com/viewarticle/833561

7 http://www.lifeextension.com/magazine/2007/10/report_depression/page-01

8 http://www.healthunits.com/news/anti-inflammatory-drugs-could-help-treat-depression

Disorders at the National Institute of Mental Health, and Clinical Professor of Psychiatry and Behavioral Sciences at The George Washington University, [9]is working to develop a Ketamine drug that won't cause negative side effects. Testing will begin next year.

- Transcranial magnetic stimulation (five sessions for thirty to forty minutes per week for four to six weeks) has been found to be helpful for mildly treatment-resistant depression.[10]
- Aerobic exercise can reduce rumination, and mildly to moderately depressed people who ran for thirty minutes and meditated for thirty minutes twice weekly for eight weeks had a forty percent decrease in symptoms.[11]

I think you will all agree these are very interesting research findings, which offer a glimmer of hope for everyone fighting the never-ending onslaught of depression.

As promised, I will conclude this blog, with a little comic relief. Without further ado, I wish you all a Happy Easter and here are the ten strangest things people have said to me:

1. "Oh, you have depression? Really? Are you sure, because you don't look depressed!"
2. "You mean you haven't been able to work for over a year because of depression? No, that can't be right. You should be over it by now. You must have something else!"
3. "Do you go to church? No? Well if you embrace the Lord, you will feel much better!"
4. "There's no such thing as depression; it's all in the mind!"

9 https://www.nimh.nih.gov/labs-at-nimh/principal-investigators/carlos-zarate.shtml

10 http://www.transcranialstimulation.com/

11 http://www.news.rutgers.edu/research-news/exerciseandmeditation-%E2%80%93-together-%E2%80%93-help-beat-depression-rutgers-study-finds/20160209#.WZs5KLpFxyO

5. "Depression? Should you be out? People who have depression are too sick to go anywhere. You must have the light version!"
6. "You can't have depression. You look too good. You are obviously high functioning!"
7. "Depression is a choice; you can choose to be depressed or not. I have never been depressed a day in my life because I choose not to be!"
8. "God will only give you what you can handle! It's a test!"
9. "Do you know how many people in the world are worse off than you? There are children starving, people dying. Really. Depression? Just get over it!"
10. And my personal favourite: "Oh no! That's not good. Satan is inside you! You invited Satan into your life; that's what depression is!"

Aah! Yes! If only it was that easy, not only would I be depression-free; so would the other 3.2 million Canadians fighting this accursed illness.[12]

---

12 The Canadian Mental Health Association. www.cmha.ca

17

April 22, 2017

A Reason to Live

This post, albeit difficult to write, and likely difficult for everyone to read, is about a dark, scary friend that has accompanied me throughout my journey with depression. The friend is *Death by Suicide*, or, as I like to call him, DBS.

In the past few weeks, it seems every time I turn on the television to watch the news, there is another story about a life ended by suicide: an 11-year-old boy from Michigan, a 21-year-old student in New Delhi, the "Facebook" killer, and most recently, a former NFL football player. While the reasons for each suicide are glaringly different, the sad reality is they all decided life was not worth living, and instead, chose to end their life, their existence on this earth.

Since hurtling down the rabbit hole 610 days ago, I have lived with that threat, that possibility, that option, that hope, that choice.

There are some who say suicide is an easy way out; a sign of weakness; a sign of cowardice; a sin against God; a selfish, thoughtless decision. I cannot speak for all those who have ended their life by suicide, but for me the decision to end one's life takes enormous strength and courage. It is not an easy way out when one makes that final decision. *It is the only way out,* the only way to escape the constant pain, emotional torture, and suffocating darkness that permeate every cell in one's body, every thought in one's head, every moment of one's existence.

In thirty-four years of nursing, I have accompanied hundreds of people on the final leg of their life journey. I have studied death and dying. I have performed first and last offices on the deceased. I have tried to understand the whole concept of death: one minute you are here, and then you are gone. And despite my experience and education, what I know with certainty is that death scares the living bejeebers out of me, and I really do not want to die!

And so, you must be asking yourself, why then, is the thought of suicide such a big part of my life? The answer is simple. I have depression. Living every second of every day with depression is like walking on a tightrope: it takes every ounce of strength and energy to maintain balance on the tightrope and to keep putting one foot in front of the other.

It is not uncommon upon hearing that someone has committed suicide for people to say, "Oh, but he/she had so much to live for." Or, "How can he/she do that to the loved ones?"

I think what people do not understand is that a person considering suicide really believes there is nothing left to live for, that the family will be better off without him or her. I have read many articles and books about suicide and depression, and almost every person has either told someone or written in their final note, "It's not that I want to die, but I cannot live with this pain," or, "I don't want to die, but I cannot deal with the demons in my head."

I completely understand how they must have felt. Every day I grieve the loss of me, myself, the person I used to be. Every day I try to rebuild my life. Every single day I fight. I fight to find myself. I fight to reclaim my life. I fight to escape the rabbit hole, and every single day I fight not to die. I fight to live!

What people need to know about depression is that it robs you of your life, your identity, your passion, your time, your present, your hopes and dreams. It robs you of your heart and soul, the very essence of your being. And, once it's sucked all the life essence from you, a shroud of darkness and hopelessness; despair and helplessness; worthlessness and grief; and intense, excruciating pain descends upon you, suffocating you, trapping you, torturing you.

So, as you read this post, I would like you to consider these questions:

- Could you live like this every single day?
- Could you continue every single day knowing there is a chance you may never get better?

I wonder what your response will be. Because I ask myself those questions every single day! How do I continue? I make a plan, not a plan to die by suicide, but rather a plan to live. It is almost like an "if all else fails" plan.

For example, I tell myself to keep going for another day, or two weeks, or three months, or six months or one year. And then, if there is no improvement in my depression, in my life, then I can end the pain and suffering and end my life: Death by Suicide!

I agree that it sounds horrible, and yes, it is strange. But it works, because when I experience those really bad days, when I do not think I can go on living, then I remember my plan, and it gives me a reason to keep going, a reason to live! And so, I pick up the oar and start paddling again, toward that dot of land in the middle of the ocean.

Since falling down the rabbit hole, I have made many plans. And here I am. It is Day 610, and I am still paddling, and I will continue to paddle for now, because I have a reason to live.

"On particularly hard days when I feel that I can't endure, I remind myself that my track record for getting through BAD days is 100% so far."[13]

---

[13] Reprinted with permission from Marcandangel@marcandangel.com

18

April 29, 2017

When Is Enough, Enough?

Today, I read a heartbreaking obituary of a 57-year-old man, who, after a "very long and arduous battle with depression" decided he could no longer continue to live with the constant pain and agony. He leaves behind a loving wife, a son, a daughter, his father and sister. The obituary reads: "Depression is someone that has everything that anyone could ever want and yet feels they have nothing to live for."

I read those words and I cried. I cried for the man, I cried for his family, I cried for every person who has suffered with or is suffering from depression, and I cried for me.

Seven days ago, that man decided *enough is enough*. Having the love and support of his family was not enough. And so, it begs these questions:

- If you have no family to love and support you, is it even possible to escape the darkness of the rabbit hole?
- If you have "everything" and cannot escape, what chance do you have if you have "nothing"?
- Can anyone really escape the clutches of DBS and go on to live a happy and productive life?
- Or, do we just continue to fight the constant pain and sadness and force ourselves to carry on, to try and put one foot in front of the other, day after day, after day, after day, each step just bringing us closer to the inevitable "enough is enough" day?

I wonder if he made deals with DBS for one more week, one more month, one more year. This thing called depression is horrible. It is menacing. It is scary. It is like a parasite just eating away at your selfhood, eroding your confidence, stripping away your self-worth, annihilating your hopes and dreams. It tears at your soul, crushes your heart, and saturates your brain with darkness, extinguishing the light of your inner being.

Presently, I am still on my raft adrift in the ocean. I continue to paddle, and I feel that I am getting a little closer to the land I see in the distance. I only hope I get there before my Enough Is Enough Day.

19

May 9, 2017

Monsters Don't Sleep Under Your Bed; They're Awake in Your Head!

Will this darkness ever end?

I feel like I am forever battling a force so powerful, so dark, so menacing; and just when I think I am winning, I awaken to a sunshine-filled morning, only to find that sometime during the night, DBS snuck in and dressed me in my cement boots and shoulder pads! His very presence is stifling, terrifying; he just won't quit!

And so, today, I must set down the oar, lie back in the sunshine, and let my raft drift a little off course.

I will not fight, or scream, or cry. I will not berate myself or listen to the monsters of depression raging in my head.

Today, I will not surrender to DBS; today is just going to be one of "those" days and tomorrow will be better!

> *"The soul always knows what to do to heal itself.*
> *The challenge is to silence the mind."*
> *- Caroline Myss[14]*

14Excerpted from her book, *Invisible Acts of Power*, reprinted with permission

20

May 16, 2017

When Words Cannot Express How Bad It Can Be

21

May 19, 2017

Tonight, I Go to Sleep

I know what it feels like to pray, "Dear God, take it all away."

And I pray with all my heart that DBS comes and takes me during the night.

No more tears.

No more exhaustion.

No more heart-wrenching sorrow.

No more crippling agony and paralysing emotional pain.

22

May 31, 2017

Pandora's Box Is Open

Legend has it that Pandora's box, which, incidentally, was really a jar (just doesn't have the same effect though: Pandora's jar!), contained all the evils of the world. When Pandora opened the 'box' all the evils flew out, leaving only Hope inside once she had closed it again.

Two weeks ago, after my first visit with the psychiatrist, my Pandora's box was opened too, and all the horrible, sad, painful, soul-wrenching things that have happened to me in my 53 years burst forth, like an erupting volcano, sending rocks and ash and spewing hot lava into my brain, debriding every hemisphere (there are 2), every lobe (there are 4), and every neuron (there are approximately 100 billion).

It consumed everything in its path: my childhood memories, my marriage, and the death of my dogs, and culminated with 'the' workplace incident. In the space of that ninety-minute appointment, I relived all those memories, as if they had just happened, one by one, explaining what my response was and how I felt.

When the appointment was over, I felt like I was having an out-of-body experience. I was dazed, confused, beaten, and exhausted. I couldn't think. I couldn't even process what was going on around me. I just sat in the car, immobile, inert, and invisible.

Experiencing a brain debridement was like nothing I have experienced before. After reliving all those memories, it felt like every part of my brain had been burned and then ripped out of my skull, leaving fresh, raw brain matter. The emotional pain was so acute, so intense, and so present, that I didn't even know how to begin to deal with everything. There was no darkness or fogginess, no heaviness; instead, every thought I had was like a searing pain ripping and tearing into what was left of my brain flesh.

It was almost like a kaleidoscope. I thought about my childhood and as I tried to process what happened, another memory appeared and then another and another. And before I knew it I was bouncing from childhood years to marriage years, to work event year, and all I felt was the buzzing and pain and sorrow. It was all I could do to walk, to talk, and to eat.

I felt so 'done' that I sat in the shower hugging my knees to my chest, rocking and crying while the hot, steaming water thrashed against my skin. I felt so 'done' that I went to bed, praying that I would die in my sleep and not wake up the next day. That's what a brain debridement feels like.

And so, here I am, two weeks later, and having another visit with the psychiatrist. This time, after reviewing how the past two weeks have been, some medications are discontinued, others are increased in dose, and new medications are added. We talk about the brain debridement and I am told that in addition to the depression, I also have PTSD (Post Traumatic Stress Disorder) and if I have any hope of healing, then I must put all the 'stuff from my box' on the shelf and concentrate only on the *now*.

Hmmm, it sounds so easy, doesn't it? Kind of like telling someone to close the barn door after the horse has bolted, especially when I didn't open the barn door!

So here I am again, trying to put all my past memories in neat little packages and stow them for another day! Yay! So many presents to look forward to opening sometime in the future!

Please excuse my cynicism, but personally, I believe, if something isn't affecting your life, then it should be left in the box, because what I know for sure is when Pandora's box is opened, there are no pretty bow-wrapped packages inside.

And so, tomorrow I begin again. I am grabbing the oar, standing up on the raft and will begin paddling towards land (hopefully I'm not too dizzy from the new medications); because what I also know for sure is this bloody mental illness is not going to stop me from reaching land. I know there are likely a few storms ahead and some rough water, and I know that the great white shark (DBS) will be staying close. But I sure as hell am not going down without a fight! :)

"Repeat after me: My current situation is not my permanent destination."
- Anonymous[15]

---

[15] tinybuddha.com

23

June 26, 2017

Where Has the Time Gone?

It must be approximately one month since my last post and six weeks since I first met with the psychiatrist. On Wednesday, I return for my third visit; apparently, it's going to be every two weeks for the foreseeable future.

I know why I must do this, but reopening old scars with a dull and rusty knife is starting to take its toll on my already battleworn and weary brain and body. The positives are that the new medications, adjusted for the third time, appear to be having a good effect. I am sleeping better but now awaken at 4:30 every morning and am usually up and drinking my coffee with the birds between 5:00 and 7:00 a.m. I think they are rehearsing for *America's Got Talent* because their chirping, cawing and tweeting is so loud it's difficult to just sit there and think. This may be a good thing, especially as I am a thinker, which is not always a good thing with a torn and tattered mind!

Life is pretty much the same routine: riding my bike for about two hours; doing errands; journaling; reading; writing my dementia articles; making doctors' visits, psychologist visits, psychiatrist visits; oh, and picking up my prescriptions every two weeks! Whatever happened to the old way, every three months? Well, I guess I shouldn't complain. At least it's no longer weekly!

Generally, I think there are more good days than bad days, and on the good days, I actually start to feel a little like the old me!

But then, as life is with depression (or should I say PTSD, due to the acute depressive episodes?), I cannot sit on my laurels too quickly because DBS is never far away. Some days, I wake up on the raft and he's right there, the fin gliding through the water, so close I can almost feel his sandpaper-like skin. And then there are days when I can be paddling away and suddenly feel a sense of heaviness, darkness, overwhelming sadness and hopelessness descending. There is no rhyme or reason why it *appears*, but when it does, I can feel my entire body deflate, that feeling of "Oh no, not again!"

I try not to fight too hard or surrender. I just try to keep going and tell myself it will pass and tomorrow will be better. I have come to the realization I will never truly be rid of this illness. Life is full of ups and downs, and everyone has bad days; unfortunately, my bad days can be a little more challenging.

Today is a not-so-good day, but I am keeping busy trying to occupy my mind and focus on other things.

If I look out of the corner of my eye, he's still there in the distance, just biding his time.

What surprises me is that even after two years, it still feels surreal, surreal but less painful. I've worked through the anger, revenge, confused, and desolate stage; and I've chosen to forgive (not in the complete biblical sense) and move on. I recognise I cannot waste any more energy trying to rectify what happened, because life goes on. In the whole scheme of things, it happened, it was horrendous, but I'm still here! And karma is a bitch! LOL!

Last Saturday, I celebrated my 30th year of living in Canada: amazing, 30 years. And sadly, for some people, that is their entire lifetime. So, I will end this post by sharing my thoughts on the past two years.

Despite the pain, sorrow and other emotional experiences with which you are now all familiar, I feel that what happened, and has happened since then, are blessings in disguise. They are a gift, an unexpected gift, for sure, but still a gift. They have opened my eyes to what is really important in life; allowed me to appreciate the simple things; reawakened my passion for writing and for dementia care; and enabled me to try to live life *in the moment* and not focus on one week, three months, or one year down the road.

24

July 7, 2017

The Sun Has Almost Set

It's a beautiful evening outside, the sun has started its descent into the horizon and even with the pervading smokiness from all the forest fires, it is bright and glowing a fiery copper orange. On evenings like this, everything appears bathed in happiness, peace and joy; I guess you could say it is almost a spiritual experience.

Unfortunately, time is slipping away at an alarming rate, and with less than four months left until my DBS contract date, I feel it is time to start bringing my blog to an end.

My last visit with the psychiatrist was surreal/unreal. I actually left her office in a worse state then when I arrived and returned home in the pouring rain, only to sit for hours and contemplate whether I just end everything then and there. As you can see, I decided to fight back. Unfortunately, the experience set me back, and so, once more, I had to go to battle and fight my inner demons.

On a positive note, I am making a complaint to the College of Physicians and Surgeons; however, the thought of having to see her again makes me feel sick to my stomach.

I guess the best way I can describe how I have been feeling these past few weeks is *battle weary*. Even though I know I have moved into a different stage of the recovery process, I feel absolutely exhausted all the time; every joint in my body hurts; I sleep for only two to four hours; I awaken with horrible, pounding headaches every morning; and while my emotional brain feels okay, it seems that all the anger, sadness and blackness has moved from my brain into my body and is trying to force its way out through my joints.

Every bike ride is a chore. It is as if I am fighting against every muscle, every sinew in my body, pleading with them to move and stop the pain. The textbooks say this is a "normal" stage of PTSD.

According to my psychiatrist, I am not doing enough to get over my depression and she accuses me of not taking my medications, of just sitting at home, doing nothing and perseverating on all that is bad in my life. Ha! ha! She has absolutely no idea, and as she is unwilling to listen to everything I have done and am presently doing, I feel like I am in a lose-lose situation.

Anyway, I digress. The purpose of this blog is to give you a quick update and to let you know that I have found an editor who is going to help me translate the words in this blog into a book. :)

I understand I will not be the next Stephen King, but if my story can help people understand what living with depression is like, and those living with depression to know they are not alone and not going crazy, then I am happy and feel I have done a good thing.

25

July 16, 2017

Sometimes I Just Wish

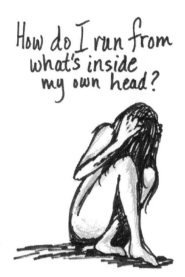

How do I run from what's inside my own head?

Sometimes, I just wish I could cocoon myself and disappear. Wrapped up tight, nice and warm, hidden away from the outside world, hidden away from life itself.

Sometimes, I just wish I could scream and scream and scream and let all the bad stuff and pain and tortuous voices in my head explode into nothingness.

Sometimes, I just wish all those who did me wrong and hastened my descent down the rabbit hole would get what they deserved.

Sometimes, I just wish I could escape this thick, suffocating cloud of darkness that follows me around.

Sometimes, I just wish I could wake up and the past two years never happened.

Sometimes, I just wish I could kick, and punch and claw myself out of this rabbit hole of hell.

Sometimes, I just wish this would all be over.

And sometimes, I just wish that wishes came true.

26

July 26, 2017

Just When I Thought It Was Safe
to Go Back in the Water

Life is funny, life is strange, life is full of surprises; don't you think? Here I am, paddling away towards a distant land, trying to keep distance between DBS and me, when out of nowhere appears a rogue wave. For those who are not familiar with the term, a rogue wave is a large, unexpected and suddenly appearing wave that is extremely dangerous, as it can impact any object in the water with tremendous force. Well, today, I encountered a rogue wave!

So, let's set the scene. There I am, paddling away in a seemingly calm, azure ocean, the sun warming my back, a cool breeze gently caressing my face, when out of nowhere appeared a rogue wave. This rogue wave was totally unexpected and for a moment almost knocked me off balance and into the ocean, into the jaws of the great white shark, DBS. Somehow, I remained upright, and after recovering from the initial shock, I forged ahead, paddling towards that distant land on the horizon, determined not to let DBS sense my weakness and make his move.

Apparently, my employer, or should I say *former* employer, because I will never ever work for them again, contacted LTD (Long Term Disability) and told them I was, in fact, working and making money that I was not declaring! Hmmm, I wonder how they came to that conclusion? Well, I guess they decided that the dementia articles I post on *Castanet* constitute paid journalism, even though it is entirely voluntary and completely free.[16]

---

[16] Refer to "Dementia Aware: What you need to know" at www.castanet.net.

But wait! There's more! Apparently, I am also a paid dementia speaker! Now, I know the articles are visible to anyone who views *Castanet*, but the information about my town hall presentation (note singular, meaning *one* presentation, not many, as was inferred) with Dan Albas, MP, was only shared with a few people, and somehow my employer was privy to specific information about that presentation. Hmmm, I wonder how that happened? I wonder how they were privy to this information? I wonder.

Life is just a maze of puzzles and conundrums, don't you agree? Anyway, the good thing is I survived the rogue wave; in fact, I didn't even fall off the raft and into the shark-infested ocean. Despite the pathetic, malicious, ludicrous, nasty, malevolent attempts by my employer (former employer, that is) to ruin my day, my week, my life, I did not fall back down the rabbit hole, not even for a nanosecond. And to the person who felt the need to talk about me: *Shame on you!* I am not angry. I am not mad. I just feel disappointment and sadness, because you know what they say. Karma is a *bitch*!

27

August 20, 2017

731 Days Down and Only 46 More to Go!

Ants in the Brain

I cannot believe today marks the second anniversary of my descent into the rabbit hole. 731 days of darkness, sorrow and fighting my inner demons. 731 days of trying to rebuff the advances of DBS. 731 days of searching for an escape route out of the rabbit hole. And 731 days of trying to find the new me, of trying to reclaim my life, of trying to accept that sometimes life completely sucks and there's absolutely nothing I can do about it.

I had thought this entry was going to be a happy, positive blog, full of hope and joy, sprinkles and fairy dust and all that fluff! If I had written it one week ago, two weeks ago, even four days ago, then it would have been just like that. But instead, after so much time spent working so hard to move forward, to change my life's purpose, to head in a new direction full of hope and possibility, in a mere three days, it can all fall apart, and here I am, clutching my third box of Kleenex (apparently two-year anniversary is paper!) and dangling my feet into the rabbit hole.

My brain is swimming with ANTs: automatic negative thoughts, fire red, poisonous, nasty ants.[17] They are everywhere, spreading their poison into my brain, tearing open the areas that have healed in place. There is just no letting up; in fact, I think they may be having a party in there. One bad thing I can deal with, two bad things are challenging, but five? Five are way too many! How can hope and potential and optimism and happiness and joy and good things get snatched away from me in the space of 72 hours?

How do I pick myself up and formulate a new life plan, a new life purpose, when there are only 46 days left before DBS cashes in his contract? I have no idea. I am so utterly wiped out, exhausted, deflated, disappointed, confused, bewildered, it's an effort to even try to type my thoughts.

Why do people offer so much, and then nothing, no reason, no apology, no explanation, just nothing? Why do people offer a ray of hope amidst the darkness and then extinguish the light; no reason, no apology, no explanation, nothing?

---

[17] Refer to Appendix IV for information about ANTs.

I am beginning to feel that maybe it is all for nothing, I am nothing, my life is nothing. Perhaps the lesson I am to learn after 731 days is that all there is in life is *nothing*: expect nothing, want nothing, be nothing, receive nothing.

I guess it's pretty simple; it just would have been nice if someone had told me that 731 days ago, 400 days ago, 270 days ago, 85 days ago, 4 days ago. It would have saved me a fortune in heartache, soul shredding, medications, psychotherapy and Kleenex!

28

September 31, 2017

Forever in Limbo

In Catholic theology, *limbo* is considered the "edge of Hell"! This is an interesting analogy and one I feel aptly describes my life for the past seven weeks.

I am suspended in a state of impermanence. It is a strange sensation, knowing my life is no longer under my control; my life is about to enter a new realm of which I know nothing. I liken it to being suspended on a hoist that is dangling my body over the rabbit hole, and the hoist is turning so very slowly I do not know if I am going to be lifted out of the rabbit hole or released into the deepest, darkest cavern from which there is no return. I am in *limbo*!

Being in a state of limbo, is quite interesting really. There is no sense of fear or anxiety, no sense of peace or joy, just a sense of nothingness.

It sounds odd to say that I feel nothing because I am not numb or inert. I still feel pain, I still cry; but I feel nothing, no sadness, no despair, no dark thoughts. I have no sense of foreboding, I have no death wish. I just feel empty, tired, beaten down. I feel like I'm very slowly losing my sense of self.

It seems, since my visits with the psychiatrist, my brain cannot heal. Too much bad stuff was ripped out at one time, and even though I have worked through most of it, there is no place to return it to be stored in my memory bank. The scars left behind are so fissured and gnarled and bruised that my brain can only hold onto so much information.

So much has happened in such a short span of time, it is overwhelming; and what initially appeared to be positive, wonderful things offering me potential and hope for the future soon revealed themselves as nothing more than false promises, bullshit and hot air. And let me tell you, all that, along with another betrayal, work crap (oh yes, they're back) and union crap, and my poor brain, fighting so hard to heal and improve, just said *enough*, and another light switch flicked off.

For those of you who do not know, the first time I ever experienced the light switch sensation was October 2012 when my beloved dog Tag died. I literally felt something change in my brain when he took his last breath.

So now, fast forward five years later, and once again I felt it happen. What does it mean? I have no idea! I think it may be my way of handling too much sadness, stress and pain. I don't know, but what I do know is it feels like a life source, an energy source is extinguished; and so, given that I have so few active positive cells firing in my depressed and traumatized brain, it feels like there are only a few more left before all the lights are extinguished.

That does not mean I am suicidal. I certainly have no intention of honoring my contract with DBS on October 4, 2017. I have no thoughts of ending it, because I feel that date has already been decided and I have absolutely no control.

Nothingness is so difficult to describe. My life continues every day, I follow the entrenched routine I set for myself long ago to keep busy, to keep sane. I smile and nod and say *hello* and go about my day, feeling nothing.

Two years of emotional torture and pain, two years of fighting DBS, of pushing ahead, of climbing back out of the rabbit hole over and over again, and for what? To try and win a war that had been won before I even arrived on the battleground? It's like being a knight on horseback, bedecked in all the garb, weapon at hand, charging into battle, surrounded by a dense mist, and I keep charging and fighting and resting and charging and fighting. And then, when the mist clears, all I see is barren landscape and a rabbit hole and nothing else.

I've spent the past two years going around in circles, fighting an invisible enemy that exists only in my mind! Yes, I am completely and utterly exhausted and just plain done. So what else is there to do but dismount, lay down the weapon, remove the battle armour and wait?

Whatever is going to happen has already begun and I can't fight it. I can't bargain with it. All I can do is wait, in limbo, and hope I'm not going to plunge down into the "nether reaches" of Hell.

29

September 29, 2017

Five More Days

Well, here I am. September 29, 2017, and the countdown is on; five more sleeps left before DBS (Death by Suicide) is supposed to come calling, contract in hand!

I cannot believe almost one year has gone by. It's true what they say: the older you get, the more quickly time passes. Did I think I would be here, today, writing this message? No! Not really. I thought I would have surrendered to DBS long ago. So, does this mean I am healed, cured, over it, depression-free? The answer is *no*!

The fact is depression is a *bitch*! it is an accursed, meddling, horrible, nasty illness that never completely leaves me. Yes, with a number of medication changes (the last one of which was only five weeks ago), and with a lot of energy, commitment and determination, I kept going, pushing forward, falling back down, forcing myself to get back up.

Yes, there are good days; in fact, there are some really good days, when it seems everything is finally over and all is good with the world. But then, just as I relax and start dreaming of a future, *bam*! Without warning, the darkness appears and once again I feel those cement boots and shoulder pads weighing me down.

You see, what they don't tell you is this: when you experience a really bad depression that goes on, and on, and on, chances are, you will also meet Depression's cousin Anxiety and her father, PTSD. And let me tell you, these family members are quite dysfunctional.

So even when the depression cloud of darkness appears lighter, and the sadness less intense, my life is infused with unexpected and, at times, overwhelming feelings of anxiety and fear that can immobilize me. Any attempt at formulating some semblance of a plan for the future results in an increased heart rate, heaviness in the chest, tightness in the throat, finger tremors and shakes. I feel clammy and my eyes are unable to focus. At times, I feel like I will faint. Fortunately, the buzzing in my brain enables me to try to focus until the symptoms subside.

But wait! There's more! Let's not forget PTSD, who arrives bearing more than one gift. He comes with an armful: pain, soreness, aching in every muscle and joint in my body, constant headaches, dizzy spells and nausea. Some days, I can hardly move it is so bad. And on the really dark *rabbit hole* days, the pain doesn't just throb and pulsate; it vibrates and twists and turns and screams from every fibre of my body.

And so now, in between visits to the doctor, psychologist and massage therapist, some new players have joined Team Tracey: a physiotherapist and a sports medicine doctor plus another change of antidepressant. Goodbye, Wellbutrin (seven percent adverse effect is arthralgia/myalgia) and hello, an increase in Cymbalta, my one constant, my one friend who has been with me since I fell down the rabbit hole!

Will this ever end?

Five more days to go. Five more days. I can hear the clock ticking.

I can hear the hoist start, and I slowly start to sway over the rabbit hole.

30

October 2, 2017

How Can One's Life Be Measured in 28 Hours?

Do you ever sit and think about your life?

- *What have you accomplished?*
- *What have you done to make the world a better place?*
- *Would you have done anything differently?*

If you were told you only had a mere 28 hours left to live, would the answers to these questions remain the same, or would they change?

I have pondered my life since I was a child. It may sound strange, but I had mapped out my life's course before I turned five years of age. I knew I was going to be a nurse, I knew I would write a book, I knew I would move away from Wales and live a new life in another country across the vast ocean. I knew I would leave my family behind.

At that time, the United States was all the rage. It was the place of dreams, of perfect white teeth, of skateboards and Farrah Fawcett hair. The British had a love-hate affair with Americans; Brits loved the glitz, glamour and make-believe but hated the self-absorption, brashness and sense of entitlement. They had McDonalds; we had Wimpey's. They had Snickers; we had Marathon bars. They had *Happy Days*; we had *Benny Hill*!

Anyway, I digress. I guess what I'm trying to say is that I too fell for the American dream and so from the age of eight, my plan was to live in the USA. Everyone thought I was crazy. They said it couldn't be done, but I clung to that dream for fifteen years.

Every time my father chased me up the stairs with a slipper in his hands ready to beat the living crap out of me, I clung to that dream. Every time he threatened my brother, my mother and me; hurled plates of food at us; left us stranded at the side of the road in a town hundreds of miles away from home and drove away; I clung to that dream. And every time he berated me, ridiculed me, belittled me, ignored me, screamed and shouted and swore at me, spewing words that poisoned my heart and my soul, I clung to that dream.

Fifteen years later, my dream came true: I became a nurse; I moved to Canada (moving to the USA was not that easy); and I left my family behind, forever.

Do I regret anything? Absolutely not! Would I do anything differently? No, I believe this was the path I was meant to follow, and sometimes bad things must happen for good things to occur.

My life in Canada began in Calgary, then onto Edmonton, Vancouver, and finally I settled in Kelowna. During those years (1987 – 2013) many things happened. I got married and divorced, three beautiful dogs came and went, I gained weight, I lost weight, I worked different jobs: doctors' offices, nursing home, private care, community care; I gained more weight, I lost more weight; I grew my hair long, I cut it short; I tried to learn Italian, I tried to learn French to no avail. And each day I questioned my life's purpose.

It seems funny that when I was so young, I had a very clear life plan set out, but once I achieved those goals, I never really sat down and made a new life plan.

So now, when I look back and reflect upon the last twenty-six years, and I ask myself, "*What have I accomplished? What have I done to make the world a better place?*" I can honestly say, "*I don't know.*"

Would I do anything differently? In some situations, yes, but you can't undo the past; and so all I can do is learn from my mistakes and hope I don't repeat them again.

Which brings me to the present, the here and now. Certainly, the past four years have been challenging. The last two years, as you know, have been the most difficult, traumatic and painful. I have endured days when I could not even function, days when I could not move, days when I cried so hard and so long I could no longer open my eyes, and I have endured days when it took every ounce of strength to fight off the entreaties of DBS (Death by Suicide). Believe me, fighting *not to die* is so much harder than one would imagine.

So here I am, a mere 28 hours to go, and once again it is time to ask myself those three life questions:

1. *What have I done?*
2. *What have I accomplished?*
3. *Would I do anything differently?*

31

October 4, 2017

"For Whom the Bell Tolls; It Tolls for Thee" (John Donne, 1624)[18]

It is almost midnight, the witching hour, when the world is cloaked in darkness and fear. Strange things happen at midnight: a carriage can turn into a pumpkin, horses into mice and Cinderella can lose her glass slipper and with it her Prince Charming. Scary things happen at midnight: ghosts walk the earth, Dracula awakens in search of new blood, and strangers lurk in dark alleys (or so they say, LOL!). For me, this midnight is particularly significant because it is exactly 390 days since I made 'the deal' with DBS (Death by Suicide), which means it is October 4th, my birthday!

I know he's here, waiting patiently; in fact, he's never left my side for the past 777 days! You'd think he'd get tired and give up, but that will never happen. Once he's in your life, it becomes very clear that he will never leave. Depression and DBS are a package deal, just like depression and anxiety, and depression and PTSD (Post Traumatic Stress Disorder). You see depression is the gift that keeps on giving, you may not want any more surprises, but the reality is that you have no choice. You can fight and take medications, employ counter measures and go to therapy, but once they align with the big D (Depression), get ready for the fight of your life!

_____

[18] Meditation XVII from *Devotions Upon Emergent Occasions*, www.poemhunter.com/poem/no-man-is-an-island/

So here I am, one year older and wondering: *What have I accomplished? What have I done to make the world a better place?*

I think the biggest and most important thing I have accomplished is to continue to fight every single hour of every day and not let the darkness completely take over my life, my soul, my being. I did not surrender to DBS even in my darkest, most painful moments. I kept going, and to me, that is a huge accomplishment.

I think telling my story to the world and letting people know that depression can be managed, and that there is a light at the end of the tunnel is one way that I can make the world a better place. Living with depression is not easy, but if I can do it, then others can too.

So, would I have done anything differently? Well, in hindsight, I would have trusted my instinct and not continued to see the psychiatrist after the initial visit. However, it is what it is. Her actions severely compromised my recovery and my self-confidence, but I continued to paddle my raft, and for the first time in a very long time, I can clearly see *land ahoy!*

October 4, 2017, 00:15H

Tracey 1   DBS 0

"Happy Birthday" to me!

Part II

The Roadmap of My Survival

Journal Entries

Exactly 20 days after I fell down the rabbit hole, I decided to journal. There was no specific reason why I picked up a pen and started to write my thoughts on that specific day; I just did.

Over the years, I have journaled many times, and upon reflection, it seems that whenever I was dealing with a highly stressful situation, or life changing event, the opportunity to document my innermost thoughts, feelings and fears helped me to try and make sense of what was happening to me.

The opportunity to transfer thoughts, feelings and emotions that I was experiencing, living, and fighting into words was good. It felt like I was cleansing my head and purging my soul of all the horrible, sad thoughts: "Out, damned spot! Out I say!"[19] (Yes, I'm channelling my Lady Macbeth here! Seven years of studying Shakespeare in grammar school finally paid off! Ha! Ha!)

In this section, I have included a selection of unedited entries from my journal. I hope they will help the reader get a better understanding of what my day-to-day life was like during that dark time, the struggles I faced, the tears I shed, the anger I felt, the hopelessness and sadness that I carried with me day in and day out. However, there are also entries that share the good days, days that made me laugh and smile, days that filled me with gratitude and an appreciation of life, and days that gave me the strength and hope to keep moving forward and get the hell out of the rabbit hole!

---

[19] Excerpted from *Macbeth*. William Shakespeare. 1623. Act 5, scene 1, page 2

Tuesday, September 8, 2015
It is a rainy, bleak day. School is back in session, and this means soon it will be winter and Christmas and snow and the loneliest time of the year. I am fading again, down into the darkest recess of the rabbit hole, the light is dimmer today and while I keep telling myself I will get through this, part of me is so utterly exhausted and wonders: *What is the point?* I am not living. I am merely existing, and the thought of spending every day, every week, every month like this makes me feel lifeless, inert, empty. All I want to do is close my eyes and sleep.

October 4, 2015, my birthday
This thing they call depression is excruciating, not painful or sad or lonely. Those words cannot describe the horrible intensity of this emotion. It is excruciating. I feel no hope, no joy, no light at the end. It is an endless tunnel that keeps going and going, on and on and on, and the emotional and physical pain just keeps getting worse. I cannot keep going through this. I cannot. I cannot. I CANNOT!! I am so done, so utterly completely done. I just cannot face another day of trying to keep upbeat and positive and looking my best and smiling. No more... no more... no more... I don't want to die, but I can't keep living like this. I am just so done.

November 27, 2015
I cannot believe how much I fell backwards today. Deep down I knew my WorkSafe claim would be denied, but the way they did it was so hurtful and harsh. They asked my doctor to tell me, because they were afraid I may harm myself; but, and this is so laughable, they don't think the bullying, the harassment, the false accusations, the lies, the intimidating, nasty, negative, spiteful, mean, disrespectful, condescending comments I experienced by a superior contributed to my acute depressive episode. I am lost for words. All I can do is cry.

I cannot believe I just burst into tears at the checkout of a grocery store. In fact, I have not stopped crying all evening, and what scares me the most is how deep the feelings of hopelessness are. And then of course the other scary thoughts start, and I wonder if I will ever get over this f*cking depression.

January 1, 2016. Happy New Year
I am so relieved 2015 is over, but the first day of 2016 has been a tough one. So many tears, so many thoughts of suicide; I am exhausted, emotionally drained.

Gratitude Thought: Receiving New Year texts from friends.

January 2, 2016
Only one episode of tears and less suicidal thoughts, BUT so much thought and effort needed to keep going and not ruminating on things and dragging down even further my already poor self-esteem. Read William Styron's *Darkness Visible*. It was difficult to read, but so much I could identify with. At least I know what I am feeling, experiencing, enduring, and suffering with is "depression at its worst" but normal! And maybe, just maybe, there is a light at the end of the tunnel.

Gratitude Thought: There *is* a light at the end of the tunnel.

January 3, 2016
Will this ever get better? Will I ever feel happy again? I have brief moments of peace and then *boom*! It hits me like a tsunami and the sadness and loneliness and feelings of fear hit all over again. Will this ever pass? I am trying to push ahead, making a To-Do list, going to Starbucks. Thank goodness it's therapy tomorrow.

Gratitude Thought: Received a free pumpkin loaf from barista at Starbucks.

January 7, 2016
A grey, damp, day. Waited all morning for a decision by Long Term Disability (LTD) about my claim. Despite the good news that it is approved, I feel nothing. My poor body and brain are so tense, so tight. I'm in fight-fright-flight mode.

Gratitude Thought: LTD claim approved.

January 18, 2016
Today is supposed to be the most depressing day of the year, so I have a free pass! LOL.

Gratitude Thought: Blue sky and sunshine peeking from behind the grey clouds.

January 26, 2016
Here I go. I'm back in the rabbit hole.

Gratitude Thought: Nothingness, only blackness.

January 27, 2016
Such doom and gloom, I have no energy, no enthusiasm, no nothing. My head feels so heavy and buzzes. It just buzzes. I can't think, I can't concentrate, I can't handle bright colours, I can't handle noise. I feel overwhelmed. I feel like I'm losing my mind.

Gratitude Thought: Managed to get up despite feeling terrible and having a bad headache, and made it through the day without totally succumbing to the darkness.

February 8, 2016
GUNG HAY FAT CHOY!

Gratitude Thought: Watching Downtown Abbey, a welcome distraction from the rabbit hole.

February 17, 2016
Fire ANTs in the brain, red fire ANTs![20]

February 22, 2016
Oh, a bad day, a really bad day. Couldn't even get out of bed until 1pm. Couldn't face the gym. Went back to bed at 7pm. So may tears, so many suicidal thoughts. So hard, so very, very hard.

Gratitude Thought: Darkness.

February 23, 2016
It's been six months since I last worked, six months of sadness, tears, suicidal thoughts, no hope, no dreams, no vision of the future. I feel done! Cement boots, cement shoulder pads, total weariness, sadness, helplessness, and hopelessness. Just can't keep going on like this.

Gratitude Thought: Managed to get an appointment to see the psychologist tomorrow. Hallelujah!

March 11 and 12, 2016
Worst two days since I fell down the rabbit hole. So bad, so very, very, very bad. Suicidal thoughts constantly. There is no hope for me. I must keep going. Tomorrow may be better. I just have to get through tonight and then one step at a time. Baby steps.

Gratitude Thought: Clocks spring forward tomorrow. Longer and lighter days to come.

---

[20] ANTs – Automatic Negative Thoughts, a term coined by Dr. Daniel Amen in his book *Change Your Brain Change Your Body* (1998). Potter/TenSpeed/Harmony, 480 pp.

March 24, 2016

When will I ever get a good night's sleep? Cannot believe I have been existing on two to four hours since last August. Every morning, every single morning, I wake up with neck pain and arm pain and a great big bloody headache. Having weird dreams, really weird out-of-context dreams, so strange. I wonder what my inner self is trying to tell me.

Gratitude Thought: I have running hot and cold water! I have running hot and cold water!

April 14, 2016

Another not so good night of fitful sleep and weird, weird dreams. What is going on with me? I don't know, but what I do know is that I don't like it. It's almost as if this depression is slowly entwining its way into my cells, into my life force. It feels like a fog rolling off the water, permeating everything in its path, enveloping my heart, brain and soul, infiltrating every nerve and fibre like a parasite. I think I have bought a lifetime lease on the rabbit hole.

Gratitude Thought: So many red and yellow tulips in the garden. I love tulips, so strong, so vibrant in colour but with an inner fragility. One shake and the petals fall.

April 28, 2016

Such a bad day, a very low ebb. No confidence, feeling worthless and hopeless. Very strong thought of just ending it. So many tears, heart-wrenching, soul-gutting tears. Can I just get a break? Please?

Gratitude Thought: Only darkness within, deep inside, tearing at my soul, my life force.

May 10, 2016

Dark clouds prevail. Now I'm awake at 3:30am every morning and can't get back to sleep. If I stay in bed the ANTs run riot.

Gratitude Thought: Pushed through the bike ride despite the fatigue, pain and sore legs.

May 22, 2016
I think the ANTs are on an extended vacation (in my head). Arrghh! I just want the voices to stop.

Gratitude Thought: I received a lovely bunch of pink peonies from a friend. They look so pretty in the white pitcher.

May 27, 2016
Oh! This waking up at 3:30a.m. *every* morning is exhausting. I wonder what it would feel like to have six hours of uninterrupted sleep? Think I may ask the doctor to check my iron levels again. Depression is barking at my heels. I feel sadness and true melancholy.

June 2, 2016
So tired. Dragged myself out for bike ride. Just want to crawl back under the covers. The big D (Depression) is reluctant to leave.

Gratitude Thought: I managed to ride 40km.

June 6, 2016
Well, it's been quite a day! Heading home from my bike ride and got hit from behind by a car and went head first onto gravel path and could hear and feel the impact of my helmet hitting the ground! The driver left. My left side is a mess of road rash, lacerations and bruising. My knee is badly swollen, and my pinkie finger is dislocated.

Gratitude Thought: Thank goodness, I was wearing my helmet. Could have been much worse.

June 13, 2016
Brutal sleep. This concussion, along with the big D, is wearing me out. So tired and sore, still.

Gratitude Thought: Watching the grey clouds disappear and a blue sky appear after the rain shower, all the spiders' webs are sparkling with raindrops.

June 24, 2016
Twenty-nine years in Canada. Wow. Surreal.

July 1, 2016
Happy Canada Day! It's a holiday here. I feel nauseous and depressed but got my sh*t together and went downtown to meet friends for a late lunch.

Gratitude Thought: Blue cheese stuffed dates and champagne. Yummy!

July 4, 2016
Happy Independence Day!
Score: 3-4
Decided to start scoring each day on a scale of 1 to 10, to see if there is a pattern to the number of really bad days I have compared to any good days. I need to see if there is a precipitating factor, because having a good day and then plummeting to the depths of Hell the next day is even worse and more exhausting and soul wrenching than three consecutive bad days.
0 = dead
1 = DBS
2 = very bad
3 = almost that bad
4 = not quite as bad
5 = neutral
6 = okay
7 = pretty good
8 = really good
9 = amazing
10= healed!

July 9, 2016
Score: 5-6
Trying not to listen to the red ANTs in my brain. Think it may be time to call it a day. I'm not strong enough to keep fighting this.

July 13, 2016
Score: 3-4
Damn it, damn it, damn it! What is wrong with me? I am so close to being done. 60 days and counting!

Gratitude Thought: Beautiful display of flowers in the garden across from me: pink, orange, white, red. Just spectacular! I love flowers.

July 14, 2016
Score: 2
A sad day in France. What happened today in Nice is so horribly sad and I feel guilty even being so depressed today.

Letter to Self[21]

Only I am responsible for my happiness, my life. There is no magic switch, so stop looking or hoping; it's all about attitude. My attitude and response to all that happens to me and around me.

Tracey, you are your own worst enemy! What do you want out of life? Do you want to lift yourself up and move forward? Or, keep putting yourself down? Make a decision!

Compliment yourself when things go well; never wait for others to compliment you. Tracey, you must start loving yourself. It's time to start feeling compassion for you.

You must care for yourself and take care of yourself, for no one else will do it. Start loving yourself now. It's all about choice, not what you do, but why you do it! Real growth can only come when you realize and accept that only you are responsible for your happiness, your life. No one else.

Now is the time to start to encourage you, to dwell on the good stuff and future possibilities. Stop ruminating, stop overthinking, get rid of those red poisonous fire ANTs in your head. You can do so much more than you think you can. Believe it!!

Tracey, you are a smart, caring, funny, kind, thoughtful woman; you are strong, sexy and beautiful.

---

[21] Inspired by this book: Newman, M., Berkowitz, B., and Owen, J. (1973). *How to Be Your Own Best Friend*, Ballantine Books, New York: NY

Remember all that you have gone through the past fifty-two years. You must have been strong, because you are still here! Remember, real growth can only come from within, and to become the person you want to be, you must use your feelings, your intuition, your intelligence and your will power, your whole self! And, if you do, the payoff will be enormous; believe it!

Sadly, up until now, you have created a kind of working hypothesis, which says: This is what life is about. *The problem is that most of the important ideas about life you have been carrying around since childhood and early adulthood, and your reactions to people, events, etc., are linked back to that inner novel you started writing as a child. Consequently, the way you react and the result you get, confirms what you have always expected, and that is neither correct nor true.*

Things that happened 30, 40 and 50 years ago are over and done with; and if you continue to let them shape your present and future life, then nothing will change. You will keep doing the same thing over and over and feel more angry and disappointed when you get the same results! Something has to give!

Remember, Tracey, life is not fair. Shit happens, and bad things happen to good people, but there's nothing you can do about it. Sometimes, Tracey, you cannot even the score; instead, you must let go and move on. Stop giving up your life on things you cannot change. You were born free, but somehow you have encased yourself in chains, and now you must let go of the chains and move on with your life.

You fear being alone until you die, but being alone as an adult can also help you to grow, to get to know yourself, to develop your powers, to become even stronger. It may not seem like it, BUT YOU CAN SURVIVE BEING ALONE, and when you own your separateness, your integrity, then and only then will you grow and be truly happy.

Unfortunately, the tragedy of having a bad childhood is that it has become your life. You have gone through life looking back at something you wish you had, or thought you should have had, instead of looking at the joy and happiness you could have today. Of course, moving forward will be very hard. It means taking chances and maybe doing things that are scary and uncertain and not knowing what the end result will be.

Your old mantra was: Between grief and nothing, I'll take grief.[22] *Now, your new mantra should be:* Between grief and a full life, I'll take a full life!

Yes, the first few steps will be scary, lonely, hard and even painful; but remember, you have been alone/lonely for most of your life. And all the losses and horrible things that happened to you happened in the past. That was then. You can't change anything, and instead you should be concerned only about NOW. Holding onto things that have already happened is futile; it is unrewarding and a waste of time and energy.

C'mon, Tracey, what if there is something infinitely more exciting waiting for you? Isn't that so much better?

---

[22] Inspired by William Faulkner's *The Wild Palms* (1939), via www.IZquotes-com/quote/228273

Tracey, stop being so unkind and unfriendly to yourself. Stop reacting. Think first. Allow yourself time to grieve, cry, get mad, then move on, one step at a time. You can do it! You can!

You know what you want out of life. You want love, to be in love, to feel love, to be loved. But right now, it is not here; and how you feel about yourself when there isn't someone around to receive and return your love will have a lot to do with how rewarding the experience of love is when you do have it.

This is going to be a big job, Tracey. It is going to take lots of patience and thought and effort to shake free of these bad habits. It will take a lot of perseverance. Try and try again. Keep going. Keep moving forward. Talk to yourself, explain things, reassure yourself, pay attention and ask yourself, "What do you want to do? Go up or fall down?" Only you have the power to make that decision. Remember, when you lapse, and you will (nobody's perfect), don't give up. Don't become a victim.

Just try to understand why it happened and steer yourself back on the right path. You are your own best friend, you and only you! So be kind to yourself. You only get one chance at this game of life.

Yes, there will be pain and difficulty and loss. But, there will also be happiness and joy and peace, if you are willing to take a chance. Tracey, be kind to yourself, love yourself, trust in yourself. You have so much to share, so much to give. Life is too short. Now is the time. Go for it. Take that first step. Take a chance. The world is waiting for you.

Tracey Maxfield, 2016

More Journal Entries

July 26, 2016
Score: 6-7
A better day, a better sleep, a good bike ride.

Gratitude Thought: Watching the horses frolicking and galloping and neighing in the field as I rode past on my bike.

August 9, 2016
Score: 6
In Phoenix, Arizona, visiting John and Donna. Really hoping the darkness doesn't overwhelm me. Flew into a crazy thunderstorm as we descended into Phoenix, so much turbulence. Amazingly, I was not freaked out (normally I would be). I was so calm. I guess that's what depression does to your psyche: you don't give a shit whether you live or die!

Gratitude Thought: Wow, I forgot how cheap alcohol is here!! Come to Mama!

August 22, 2016
Score: 2-4
Wow, it's been an entire year since I last worked! An entire year since my mind completely detached itself from my body, my soul, my life, my everything. It feels surreal and then, at the same time, it also feels like a lifetime ago. Tears, bad thoughts, and that pervading sense of hopelessness and helplessness are taking over again. Just try and make it to September 9, 2016. It may get better. It must.

Gratitude Thought: An amazing rainbow over the lake, set against the backdrop of the mountains. Nature's beauty at its finest.

August 25, 2016
Score: 6, initially; but 2 by 7pm
A sad day. A dear friend just lost his beloved dog. Brought back
so many memories of Tag and Piper. Ah… dogs, such great pets.
Unconditional love: the best.

September 2, 2016
Score: 4
And that's pushing it. Despite venturing out to run a few errands,
I'm so tired. My feet are encased in cement and I just feel done,
so bloody done.

September 9, 2016
Score: 6
Hooray! The horrible twelve-year cycle I have been trapped in is
over, and now I am supposed to have the best year ever! So, let's
try again and rid my life of this accursed monster Depression
and his accomplice DBS.

September 15, 2016
Score: 7
A lovely day, full of nice and unexpected surprises: wine and
sushi for lunch and went to a great movie called *Don't Breathe*.
And the weather was perfect: sunshine, blue sky and autumn
leaves.

September 23, 2016
Score: 5
A blah, grey day. So teary this morning, not sure if I can get
through this!

Gratitude Thought: A cold and brisk ride in the rain.

October 4, 2016
Score: 7
My birthday, today at 23:45. I turn 53 years old. 53! Where has time gone; where has my life gone? Almost thirty years in Canada, divorced three years. Life is strange, always changing, never boring and yet it has its moments of awesomeness.

Gratitude Thought: I am still alive.

October 17, 2016
Score: 6
A not so good sleep. Tense, anxious, feel so tight. Needed half an Ativan to relax. What is wrong with me? Just feel like I'm waiting for the shoe to drop!

Gratitude Thought: Only taken me forever, but I finally managed to clean all three bathrooms.

October 30, 2016
Score: 5
Mood taking over again. Angry, tired, fed up. Arrghh! When will this Hell end?

Gratitude Thought: Invitation for lamb dinner and red wine from a good friend.

November 10, 2016
Score: 6
Today I feel like I am totally alone in this universe and no one loves me, not even a dog! No one, and no one ever will! Wow, Pity Party Tracey!!

Gratitude Thought: Tomorrow is Remembrance Day.

November 20, 2016
Score: 5/6
Bored and weather yucky. Can't risk the ANTs in the brain, so dragged out the boxes of Christmas decorations and started to decorate.

Gratitude Thought: Nothing like twinkling lights to enliven one's mood and create magical thoughts.

November 25, 2016
Score: 6
Sick, sore throat, sore all over, tired. Feels like I'm coming down with something. Gotta keep busy.

Gratitude Thought: Unbelievably beautiful outside. Sunshine, clear blue sky, brisk cold and frosty. It looks like Christmas.

November 30, 2016
Score: 7
Made decision to write blog about this infernal depression, as Dr. K. suggested. Texted a few friends to ask their thoughts and all are supportive. So tomorrow it will be *bare all and tell all* time! Who knows what will happen? Good things, maybe? I am feeling very positive about doing this.

Gratitude Thought: Chocolate, chocolate, chocolate... After eighteen months of not eating chocolate I relented and ate some! Delicious, yummy, decadent! I don't care what anyone says, once you eat it again, the cravings start all over.

December 1, 2016
Score: 8
Blog is up and running. Invited ten friends. I feel like this could be the start of something, a change for the better! Don't want to get ahead of myself, but I feel so proud. This feels awesome!

Gratitude Thought: Figured out my blog on my own, despite the brain fog and buzzing! Yay!

December 3, 2016
Score: 5
I feel okay, not great but okay. Gotta keep going, I have experienced some 'almost' normal days and I just have to keep going... keep going... keep going...

Gratitude Thought: Today I am thankful for chocolate-covered peanuts, on sale no less! Yay! And for seeing the mountains sprinkled with snow.

December 7, 2016
Score: 5
It's a really cold day... brrr. No snow. Feel so sad, tears from nowhere! Gotta keep going. I am determined not to give in or give up!

Gratitude Thought: Today I am thankful for positive and supportive comments about my blog.

December 14, 2016
Score: 3
Terrible day, despite a pretty good sleep. Really, really depressed mood and tears, oh so many tears; I've got to get a grip on my life, on myself, on everything.

Gratitude Thought: Despite the cold and grey gloomy day, I am so very fortunate that I can come home and sit in front of a warm fire, because it's better than living on the street, in the freezing cold.

December 20, 2016
Score: 6
Not such a good sleep but still a pretty good day despite the initial dark, sad feelings.

Gratitude Thought: I am thankful for a gorgeous, gorgeous day, blue sky, sun, fresh snow. It looked exactly like a scene from *National Lampoon's Christmas Vacation*.

December 24, 2016
Christmas Eve
Score: 5
Here we go... Ho! Ho! Ho! Eight days left in 2016 and one day to go before it's Christmas. Tough morning, but trying to focus. It's only one day!

Gratitude Thought: Today, I am thankful for a free venti eggnog latte at Starbucks, for having the strength to clean my bathroom and wash the floors!! Small things!!

December 26, 2016
Score: 5
My mood is worse today. I could feel the dark thoughts creeping back, trying to weave into my neurons... tears... tears.

Gratitude Thought: I am thankful for feeling the light feathery snow on my face, my hands, my tongue.

December 30, 2016
Score: 4
Not a good day, lots of tears, very down, bad thoughts, headache. No gym workout, so very, very tired, lonely, fed up, completely done, exhausted...

Gratitude Thought: Received a nice email from a friend wishing me an early Happy New Year.

December 31, 2016
New Year's Eve
Score: 6
Well, here we are, only hours left before we bid a final farewell to 2016 and welcome the arrival of a new year, full of life yet untold: 2017! So, so, so looking forward to this. It will be, has to be, must be my year! I have done penance, I have cried, battled and suffered, and I do believe it is my time, my final "kick at the can," as it were.

Gratitude Thought: I embrace the advent of 2017, with a clean house, a clean car, a healthy snack for supper and red wine. This is different for me.

January 2, 2017
Score: 7
Another bad headache. I feel ugh... keep feeling positive... focus...

Gratitude Thought: Today I am thankful for the magnificent, glorious day: pure blue sky, brilliant sunshine, white snow all around and on the mountains, mirror-like lake and brisk cold temperatures, pure bracing ventilation, just a beautiful winter's day.

January 5, 2017
Score: 5
Black dog at my door again!

Gratitude Thought: That I have made it through another day.

January 11, 2017
Score: 5/6
Not doing well again. Don't know why I am in this downward spiral. The weather is gorgeous. I have the whole day ahead of me and yet, I am so wound up in my darkness, I can't see possibilities and positives.

Gratitude Thought: For an icy cold, take-your-breath-away kind of day.

January 20, 2017
Score: 7
Up so very early today…. bad sleep… Made a start on 'the difficult' blog post. Thought it was pretty darn good, given the subject matter.

Gratitude Thought: Yay! I won $9.00 on a scratch card! Little things!

January 29, 2017
Score: 5
It's Sunday. What can I say? Amazing how quickly the sadness and darkness descend. I need to do some big-time self-analysis here. Really feel the loneliness today. Keep going, Tracey, keep going.

Gratitude Thought: Positive feedback about first dementia aware column post on *Castanet.*

February 5, 2017
Score: 5/6
Day 1 on Wellbutrin, Okay day.

Gratitude Thought: Starting another antidepressant to add to my cocktail of sad pills.

February 7, 2017
Score: 4/5
Day 3 on Wellbutrin. What an interesting and different day!
Good news about my dementia articles and an opportunity to
contribute to a Seniors Booklet. OMG. I'm stunned, gob smacked,
overwhelmed; and what's really sad and disheartening is that I
am so blah and unenthusiastic. I feel nothing.

Gratitude Thought: It was a really good day, but my mood is
just not responding appropriately.

February 17, 2017
Score: 5
A strange day, intensely sad and so down this morning, but did
hold it together.

Gratitude Thought: Today I am most thankful for the
opportunity to sit outside on the deck and read a book before the
clouds obscured the sun and it cooled down. Felt like
summertime, and that feeling of sunshine, blue sky and relaxing
on the deck, engrossed in a good book; it's just so heavenly.

February 26, 2017
Score: 6/7
A good sleep, a good day, mood better, didn't succumb to dark
thoughts.

Gratitude Thought: Melting snow, light until 6pm, sparse,
gnarly tree branches silhouetted against a darkening sky: pretty,
eerie, mystical.

March 1, 2017
St. David's Day!
Score: 7
Another good day. It must be the medications and, hopefully, the mindset, because the weather is icky, bleak, grey, cloudy, blah!

Gratitude Thought: No bad thoughts. I feel so much better than the last few weeks.

March 8, 2017
Score: 6
Feeling a little down, keeping focused on positives, made it through the day.

Gratitude Thought: Sitting outside on deck, feeling the warm sun on my face. So thankful for that moment!

March 10, 2017
Score: 3
Oh! What a fall, back down the rabbit hole! So much anxiety, full of fear, angst, flight-fright-fight feeling. So hopeless; so, so down; blackness, on verge of tears; bad, bad thoughts back again. I am never getting over this! Ever! I am f*@#cked!

Gratitude Thought: Watching the snow melt before my eyes. Quite amazing how a landscape can change in a matter of hours.

March 17, 2017
Happy St. Patrick's Day!
Score: 5
Feeling so-so, or, as they say in Italy, *cosi – cosi*! Finally jumped on my bike and headed out on first bike ride of the year. My legs were like jelly; thought my lungs would explode at times, but I did it! Yay! So proud of myself!

Gratitude Thought: Feeling the icy cold air on my face, I feel alive!

March 30, 2017
Score: 5
Feeling weird today, sinus headache, so very tired, and another grey blah day. Feeling like I'm slipping back down the rabbit hole. Some nice things have been happening to me and I should be so happy and joyous and instead, here I am waiting for the other shoe to drop.

Gratitude Thought: I walked around downtown Kelowna after therapy and saw some cool stores.

April 5, 2017
Score: 4
26 weeks left!
I am so unbelievably exhausted and tired. I have just got to let things be. I will not submit to the rabbit hole.

Gratitude Thought: I bought beautiful pink daisies as surprise thank-you gifts for two friends. Doing so feels good.

April 7, 2017
Score: 2
Well it happened, after fighting it all week, *bam!* Down the rabbit hole I plunged! So fast! So very fast it caught me off guard. Grey, thick heavy clouds, more rain, sodden ground and sodden heart. No ride today, so much downheartedness! Three strikes and I'm out! I fall apart. Feeling anger at myself and at the system, frustration and disappointment in myself, and let's not forget the self-loathing and brain persecution. Ha! Let's be honest; no-one does a better job at totally obliterating my sense of self than me, myself, and I!

Gratitude Thought: For keeping going...

April 17, 2017
Score: 3-4
When will this emotional torture end? Despite a good sleep and trying to keep busy, I have really struggled to keep afloat today. These endless grey skies are not helping and are dragging me down and down and down some more. I have shed some tears, thought and thought some more about *the end, my end*, and now I am just so bloody exhausted. I know for certain this will *not* end and not even shocking my brain (ECT, electroconvulsive therapy) will help. Upon reflection, I realize, quite unequivocally, that I have no reason to live! Not one person to live for! Not one reason!

What a f*cking loser I am! How did it come to this? Anyway, not quite sure what else there is to say, except for now, I must keep going, keep pushing ahead, keep hoping, keep trying, keep fighting, keep inwardly screaming!

Gratitude Thought: I kept going.

April 23, 2017
No more rating my day. I just plotted the numbers on a graph to see if there were any triggers, anything to help me figure out why I can't get over this infernal depression. The graph looked like a frigging abnormal cardiac arrhythmia. LOL! Guess that speaks volumes about the state of my head. Ha, ha, ha!

Gratitude Thought: I'm reading a good book about Henrietta Lacks. Wow!

April 30, 2017
Such a bad day, such a really bad day. I can hardly walk, I feel so weighted down by the cement boots, so exhausted, so beat up and downtrodden. Back to the tears and poor self-worth and sense of hopelessness. I AM PATHETIC! I AM TAKING CONTROL. I AM THINKING OF BRINGING MY PLAN FORWARD. NO POINT DRAGGING THE HORSE TO WATER! HE'S DEAD AND THERE'S NO WATER ANYWAY! OCT 4, 2017 IS WAY TOO FAR AWAY!

May 6, 2017

A warm and sunny day. No bike ride. I feel so sore and can feel my mood flickering to dim.

Gratitude Thought: Trying to keep positive, despite feelings of unsettled angst and no idea why?!

May 15, 2017

Not such a good day; grey, bleak, cloudy, rainy, miserable. Mood is not good but gotta push forward. Have got to make it to October 4, 2017.

Gratitude Thought: Yummy bacon-wrapped blue cheese dates!

May 17, 2017

First visit with psychiatrist. I feel absolutely battered, bruised and exhausted. Holding it together, just!

May 19, 2017

A strange day again. I feel like I am in a heightened state of angst, as I am reliving all those memories the psychiatrist had to open up and then tell me to pack them in a box and put them on the shelf, because I'm too vulnerable to deal with them right now! *WTF*! Are you kidding me? I have so many emotions swirling around in my brain: anger, despair, sorrow, sadness, bewilderment, disbelief, frustration, depression, disappointment, unfairness and intense f*cking rage! Why me? Why now? I feel so sick and sad; overwhelmed is an understatement. I would be quite happy to die right now, to fall asleep and never wake up!

May 20, 2017

Well, what can I say? I am still... I don't know... I don't know what I am anymore.

May 31, 2017
Second visit with psychiatrist. I am absolutely shattered, drained, numb, inert, immobile, and all cried out! How can she expect me to not deal with everything she brought out? She makes it sound so easy. I'll just head to Home Sense, buy myself a pretty box with coordinating ribbon and bow, pack up my troubles, leave them on the shelf and walk away!

June 14, 2017
Third visit with psychiatrist. More medication changes. I don't want to add more pills to my drug cocktail, especially pills that I can become dependent on! Feeling like she is not listening to me! We go through the same B.S. She tells me I'm too vulnerable to deal with past stuff and then keeps bringing it up. Arrghh!

June 26, 2017
Note: there was no June 25th. Started off okay and ended with a double dose of Clonazepam and a very early night! I don't think I'm going to make it!

July 9, 2017
I feel broken down; darkness is hovering really close.

July 20, 2017
It has been eleven days since I journaled, and I feel like I have been walking around in a complete fog!

The visit with my psychiatrist was so unbelievable, so completely bizarre, I am still trying to make sense of what happened. It was like she thought I was another patient and was so angry and rude and disrespectful, reprimanding me for continuing to see the psychologist, telling me journaling was a waste of time, and the crème de la crème: telling me to just go kill myself and stop wasting her time! I am completely broken. My heart, my soul, is eviscerated.

September 6, 2017

Empty pages in my journal. I just have no desire to document my thoughts daily. Only four weeks to go before my birthday. It's time to start again, get back on track, get focused. C'mon, Tracey, you can do this.

Gratitude Thought: Sunlight filtering through the leaves of a tree, a warm, gentle breeze on my face, uplifting, caressing.

September 14, 2017

Arrghh! More medication changes. Shoot me now! Bye-bye, Wellbutrin. Making me way too anxious and joint pain is really bad. Hello, my old friend Cymbalta. Time to up you to 120mg daily!

Gratitude Thought: The leaves are embracing their autumn hues: red, orange, russet brown, gold, burgundy… just lovely.

September 22, 2017

It's getting closer. It's so weird; it's been such a part of my life for so long now that I almost feel I have to do it! How strange is that? LOL!

Gratitude Thought: Sunflowers. I love sunflowers, yellow ones and orange ones.

September 27, 2017

Well, girl, this is it: the countdown has begun. One week to go! Time to decide: live or die?

Right now, I wish I could feel the effects of the increased antidepressant dose. My joint pain is a little better, anxiety better, less overwhelming and suffocating, but the darkness is always there.

Gratitude Thought: I'm still here!

October 1, 2017

I can't believe what's going on in the world. 2017 has been such a horrible year for destruction, annihilation, pain and loss. So much pain and loss everywhere! What is happening? It feels like the earth has shifted off its axis and everything is messed up: hurricanes, terrorist attacks, forest fires, nuclear war threats, earthquakes.

Gratitude Thought: That I have water, power, food, fluids, a flushing toilet, transportation and, despite my aches, pains and fractured brain, I am mostly healthy. Or so I think, ha, ha!

October 4, 2017

Happy Birthday! 54 years old today!

Gratitude Thought: I MADE IT!

My Self-Help Plan

- Take a deep breath, relax shoulders, unclench hands and repeat the phrase: "This will pass; it will get better."
- After the initial acute, in-shock, exhausting stage, get out of bed. You must get out of bed after two weeks, maximum. I had no choice. I was alone and had to drink and use the toilet, take medications and eat.
- Try to drink four to six glasses of water daily.
- Try to eat three small meals daily. Allow treats.
- Take all medications as prescribed.
- Listen to music, nothing sorrowful or very loud.
- Colour books... colour... colour... colour! Trust me; it is amazing and so therapeutic.
- Do 'easy' big print crosswords, computer games, word puzzles and jigsaw puzzles.
- Paint your toenails a bold, bright colour.
- Take a warm Epsom salts bath.
- Talk to someone who understands.
- Keep a journal: write your thoughts, fears AND express gratitude for one thing that happened the day of your entry.
- Write inspirational quotes on Post-It notes and display them around your home.
- Exercise three to five times a week: gym in winter, ride bike in summer, paddleboard.
- Weekly massage: Neck, shoulders and back.
- Watch cartoons daily. I purchased the *Pinky and the Brain* DVD series. As silly and as difficult as it may seem, you absolutely must try and smile and/or laugh, even if it's just a very, very small *ha!*
- Make lists, lots of lists: errands, groceries and things to do. I would make a list of everything I need to do every day, e.g. make bed, eat breakfast, shower, etc. Trust me; it feels so good to delete a task. Gives you a sense of purpose and a feeling of control.
- Punch pillows and cushions, scream in the shower.

- Make the bed every day, every single day without fail.
- Clean teeth.
- Take a shower daily, even if it's late in the afternoon or evening, shower!
- Do one household task daily.
- Go outside every day, if only for a minute, and breathe in the air.
- See your physician and psychologist regularly.

Books that helped me:
Darkness Visible by William Styron
Reasons to Stay Alive by Matt Haig
The Mindful Way through Depression by M. Williams, J. Teasdale, Z. Segal and J. Kabat-Zinn
Everything Happens For A Reason by M. Kirshenbaum
Open Heart, Open Mind by Clara Hughes
Change Your Brain, Change Your Life by Dr. Daniel Amen
History of a Suicide by Jill Bialosky
I Can See Clearly Now by Dr. Wayne Dyer

Website:
"Getting Back to Happy" www.marcandangel.com

Epilogue

"The best way out is always through."
- Robert Frost (1874-1963)[23]

Keeping a journal, following my self care plan, writing a letter and creating a blog helped me to keep moving forward and pushing through the depression. There is no secret recipe, no one particular thing that I did that saved me, it was a combination of several things: medications, doctor, psychologist, keeping a routine, and lifestyle choices. It certainly was not easy, and I hope I will never, ever have to go through anything like that ever again. However, I do feel very strongly, that if I had not followed my daily routine, then I would not be here, right now, writing this.

I encourage you to do what works for you, but make no mistake: you must do something. After those first two weeks of intense catastrophic sadness and darkness and pain, if you do not begin to take that first step to reclaim your life and plan your escape from the rabbit hole, then you never will. The darkness and the intense sadness and the ANTs in your brain will take over, and you will surrender out of sheer exhaustion and emotional fatigue.

I won and I was alone, completely alone. I did not think I could do it; others told me to keep going, keep going, keep going, and so ultimately, I had to make a decision. Do I fight the war or surrender? There is no middle ground, no waking up and everything is better, no single medication that will wipe it all away.

---

[23] From the poem "A Servant to Servants," *North of Boston*, 1915, Excerpted: Bartleby.com

Depression is real; when it is your reality, your life, your battle to fight. The question you must ask yourself is, "Do I want to win this war?"

I choose to fight; yes, I came close to surrendering many times, but I got back up and I kept going. I know I have not won the entire war, but I have won more than a few battles; and right now, I am okay with that.

My journey through depression will continue, and I will take it one day at a time, one battle at a time, because I know I can get through this for . . .

> "Once you choose hope, anything is possible."
> - Christopher Reeve[24]

[24] www.goodreads.com/quotes/263437-once-you-choose

Acknowledgements

For as long as I can remember, people have told me I should write a book. Over the years, I have written many books in my head, but never put pen to paper. The thought of sitting at a desk, typing endless pages of words to create a story did not appeal to me. When I turned fifty, a significant milestone in anyone's life, I wrote the proverbial bucket list, and tucked in between "learn a second language" and "visit Greece" were those familiar words: *write a book*.

Fifty turned into fifty-one and then, two months shy of my fifty-second birthday, my life as I knew it ended and I found myself plummeting head first down the rabbit hole. It took me fifteen months to climb out of the darkness and overwhelming despair and sadness, but when I finally glimpsed that small ray of light that signified hope and possibilities, I knew what I had to do. It was time to share my story, and *Escaping the Rabbit Hole* was born.

I could not have completed this journey without the kindness, patience, support and understanding of a very special group of people. Words can never express what you all mean to me. I think of each one of you as a beam of light that helped me push through the darkness and into the light.

> *Sometimes we need someone to simply be there,*
> *Not to fix anything, or do anything in particular,*
> *But just to let us feel that we are cared for and supported.*
> - Anonymous[25]

I express my heartfelt thanks and gratitude to:

Dr. Sarah Brears, for her kindness, understanding, patience and belief that I would get better.

---

[25] http://shareinspirequotes.blogspot.com/

Dr. E Kuelker, who supported me throughout my darkest moments and encouraged me to write a blog describing my journey through depression.

My gravatars, Sherri Jennens, Trish Hack, Linda Skoreyko, Perry Maxfield, Mimi Stuart, Brian Komar, Krista Kunz, and Magda Mutch, who read my blog and experienced my good, my bad, and my ugly days.

John and Donna Geissler, in Arizona, who accompanied me every step of the way as I tried to escape the rabbit hole and who knew before I did this was the book I would write.

Mark Hickman, whose roadside chats helped me to keep moving forward on the bad days. He inspired me on the good days, and despite my many tears, always made me laugh.

Victoria Brewster for convincing me my blog was book-worthy and connecting me with Julie, my editor.

Chad Krahn, Jim Pischak, Patrice Tokar, and Bronk Kvapil for just being there and knowing the right things to say.

Jeff at London Drugs for his creative solutions to assist me in paying for my Cymbalta medication.

Aunt Esther and Melanie and Stuart Eckley in Wales.

The Mission Park Starbucks baristas who always greeted me by name, knew my drink of choice (Americano misto in winter and coffee Frappuccino in summer) and not once questioned why I sat by the window every single day, working on the *National Post* crossword puzzle.

And last but certainly not least, my editor and illustrator, Julie Saeger Nierenberg (and her husband Earl), who, despite experiencing her own personal challenges, supported me, inspired me and convinced me this book was one people would want to read.

Appendices

Appendix I: Mental Health Resources

Depression:

Bell Canada Let's Talk
www.letstalk.ca

The Best Brain Possible – Debbie Hampton
www.thebestbrainpossible.com

Canadian Association for Suicide Prevention
www.suicideprevention.ca

Canadian Mental Health Association
www.cmha.ca

Canadian Network for Mood & Anxiety Treatment
www.canmat.org

Centre for Suicide Prevention
www.suicideinfo.ca

Depression and Bipolar Support Alliance
www.dbsalliance.org

Defeat Depression
www.defeatdepression.ca

Depression: Here to Help
www.heretohelp.bc.ca

Depression – The Lifeline Canada Foundation
https://thelifelinecanada.ca/resources/depression

Depression Hurts
www.depressionhurts.ca

Kids Help Phone
www.kidshelpphone.ca

LifeLine Suicide Prevention and Awareness Mobile App
www.thelifelinecanada.ca

Mental Health Services, Help and Support in Your Community
www.eMentalHealth.ca

Mind Your Mind
www.mindyourmind.ca

Mood Disorders Canada
www.mooddisorderscanada.ca

Mood Disorders Psychopharmacology Unit: Uni Health Network
www.mdpu.ca

National Network for Mental Health
www.nnmh.ca

Teen Mental Health
www.teenmentalhealth.org

Find a Psychologist:
www.psychology-canada.ca
www.findapsychologist.ca

Find a Canadian Certified Counsellor:
www.ccpa.accp.ca

Counsellors:
Talk with Family Doctor/Psychiatrist
Refer to Yellow Pages

Support Groups:
Contact Mental Health Services @ local Health Authority
Check community websites and newspapers

Appendix II: Bullying

Bullying is no longer confined to the playground. It can happen at any time, anywhere, by anyone, regardless of age, gender, ethnicity or religion. While there is increased media and public involvement to stop bullying in schools, and the recognition of Pink Shirt Day and International Day of Pink,[26] very little is said about the bullying of adults, especially in the workplace.

Being the victim of a bully can be a devastating experience and can affect every aspect of one's life; the emotional and psychological impacts can result in reduced job performance, anxiety, depression and even suicide.

According to the Workplace Bullying Institute, over one-third of people have experienced workplace bullying, and a boss, supervisor or superior instigates 72% of these incidents. In Canada, 40% of workers experience bullying on a weekly basis.[27] Adult bullies can be sly, subtle and difficult to expose; but they have one thing in common: they want to hurt someone.[28]

Bullying can be:
- Physical
- Sexual
- Verbal. This type of bullying is very common and can be so subtle. Verbal abuse is very difficult to document and usually occurs when there is no one else around. Verbal bullying includes sarcasm or demeaning comments, false allegations, cruelty, humiliation, spreading rumors, ongoing harassment, intimidation, isolation from others, and threats about job security. The bullying is deliberate;

---

[26] International Day of Pink is held every second Wednesday in April and Pink Shirt Day is held in February.
[27] Lee and Brotheridge, 2006

[28] Scheff, 2014

the goal is to gain power and control over the person and to show him or her who's boss.[29]

If you are being bullied:
- Any inappropriate physical or sexual behaviour must be reported to the police.
- Document all incidents in detail.
- Try to minimise contact with bully.
- Do not meet the bully alone; try to ensure other people are within earshot.
- If called to meet with the bully, ask the union representative or a trusted work colleague to accompany you.
- If the behaviour is escalating and impacting your personal and professional life, report it to your supervisor.
- If your supervisor is the bully, report it to upper management.
- If your employer has a 'whistleblower' policy, report the person immediately.
- Contact a union representative for support.
- Follow up with your physician.
- Talk with family and trusted friends.
- Seek counselling or psychological support.

---

[29] www.bullyingstatisitcs.org.

Appendix III: Some Interesting Facts About Depression[30]

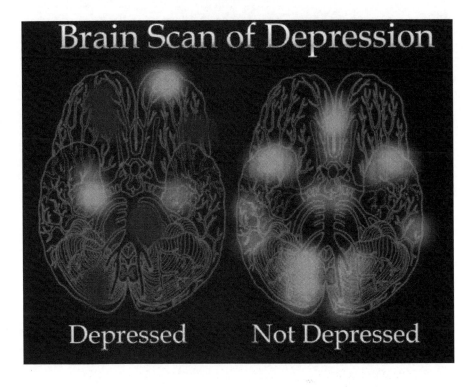

Brain Scan of Depression

Depressed   Not Depressed

Did you know that 1 in 5 Canadian adults over the age of 18 will suffer a mental disorder in their lives with anxiety and depression being the most common?

Approximately 10% of the adult population, that is 2.5 million Canadians, will have a depressive disorder in their lifetime.

---

[30] Sourced from the Canadian Mental Health Association, 2017, www.cmha.ca
[31] Permission granted by Rosemary Perry on September 29, 2017 from MCHS Permissions

A depressive disorder can affect anyone, at any age, and at any time.

A depressive episode is classified as mild, moderate or severe (acute).

The DSMMD-5 (Diagnostic & Statistical Manual of Mental Disorders) and Canadian Mental Health Association identify a number of depressive disorders:
- Major depressive disorder (including postpartum)
- Dysthymia
- Premenstrual dysphoric disorder
- Disruptive mood dysregulation
- Atypical depression
- Substance or medication induced depression
- Depression due to another medical condition
- Situation depression (stress response syndrome, formerly adjustment disorder)
- Psychotic depression
- Bipolar depression

The common feature of all these disorders is the presence of sad, empty or irritable mood, accompanied by somatic and cognitive changes that significantly affect the individual's capacity to function. What differs among each disorder is the duration, timing or presumed etiology.

On average, most people with depression will have four to five relapses (less than six months after initial treatment) and/or episodes (six months or longer after previous episode) during their lifetimes.

The most common treatments for depression are medication, psychotherapy and lifestyle changes.

Every person's experience with and treatment for depression will be different and ever changing.

Appendix IV: ANTs
Automatic Negative Thoughts

The acronym ANTs was first used by renowned clinical neuroscientist and psychiatrist, Dr. Daniel G. Amen to describe the different type of negative thoughts an individual can experience.[32]

The premise is that every time you have a thought, your brain is activated, and a chemical is released. If the thought is happy, then a chemical is released that makes you feel good; however, if the thought is bad, then the chemical that is released makes you feel unhappy.

Dr. Amen describes nine types of ANTs and offers suggestions on how to overcome the different negative thoughts with creative positive thoughts:

ANT 1 – All or nothing thoughts
ANT 2 – "Always" thoughts
ANT 3 – Focusing only on negative thoughts (red ANTs)
ANT 4 – Predicting the worst possible outcome thoughts (red ANTs)
ANT 5 – Mind reading thoughts (red ANTs)
ANT 6 – Thinking with your feelings thoughts
ANT 7 – Guilt thoughts
ANT 8 – Labeling self (or others) thoughts
ANT 9 – Blaming others thoughts (poisonous red ANTs)

The ANTs that do the most damage to a person's confidence, self-esteem and self-worth are the red ANTs 3, 4 and 5. ANT 9 is the most poisonous red ANT; it blames everyone else for problems in life and does not change anything to improve one's life.

---

[32] Source: Amen, Daniel G. *Change Your BRAIN, Change Your Life* (2015), pp. 109-113.

Appendix V: Suicide Warning Signs[33]

The Canadian Mental Health Association (CMHA) uses the acronym "IS PATH WARM" to identify the warning signs that a person may be suicidal:

I – Ideation about suicide
S – Substance abuse, e.g. alcohol, drugs
P – Purposelessness in life
A – Anxiety or feeling overwhelmed
T – Trapped, feeling there is no way out
H – Hopelessness or helplessness
W – Withdrawn from family, friends and activities
A – Anger or rage
R – Recklessness: engaging in unsafe, risky or harmful
    behaviours
M - Mood change

More subtle signs include:
- Hearing voices to kill oneself
- Getting affairs in order
- Giving away or selling belongings
- Suddenly happy and enthusiastic after a lengthy period of profound sadness
- Referencing a specific day/date in the future
- Unwillingness to make plans past a specific date
- Inviting family and friends for a social get-together

If you have suicidal thoughts:
- Remove yourself from your location, e.g. if you plan to self-harm in the bathroom, go to another room.

[33] The Canadian Mental Health Association

- Call a trusted friend or family member.
- Call a local crisis centre.
- Go to your nearest Emergency Room (ER) or call 911.

If you know someone who is expressing suicidal thoughts:
- DO NOT LEAVE the person alone.
- Call a local crisis centre and/or emergency police services.
- Take the person to your nearest ER department.
- If the person has already self-harmed, call 911 immediately.

Post Care:
- Follow up with a physician or psychiatrist.
- Consider counselling and/or participation in a support group.
- Contact the Canadian Mental Health Association, www.cmha.com, or your own local mental health branch.

Appendix VI: Post-Traumatic Stress Disorder (PTSD)

Post-traumatic stress disorder (PTSD) is a mental health condition triggered by experiencing or witnessing a traumatic event.[34] An event is considered traumatic when it is very frightening, overwhelming and causes a lot of distress.[35]

Everyone at one time or another may experience trauma. Initially, a person may have difficulty adjusting and coping, but with good self-care, the symptoms usually resolve. However, for some people, the symptoms continue.

No one knows for sure why PTSD occurs in some people and not others, but there is thought to be a connection, such as length of time the trauma lasted, number of traumatic experiences in a person's life, reaction to the traumatic event and the support the person received.[36]

Risk Factors
- Experiencing prolonged trauma
- Family history of mental health problems
- Substance abuse
- History of depression and/or anxiety
- Ineffective or no support system
- History of traumatic experiences, e.g., childhood abuse
- Frequent exposure to high-risk traumatic events, e.g., first responders, hospital staff, military personnel[37]

---

[34] Mayo Clinic, www.mayoclinic.org/diseases-conditions/post-traumatic-stress-disorder/symptoms-causes/syc-20355967

[35] The Canadian Mental Health Association (CMHA), https://cmha.ca/documents/post-traumatic-stress-disorder-ptsd

[36] Ibid.

[37] Mayo Clinic, www.mayoclinic.org/diseases-conditions/post-traumatic-stress-disorder/symptoms-causes/syc-20355967

Symptoms

Symptoms can occur months or even years after a traumatic event and can affect a person's ability to function daily.

Symptoms of PTSD can also cause problems in social and work situations and in personal relationships.

Symptoms can vary over time and can be exacerbated during stressful times or when reminded of the event.

Having PTSD may also increase a person's risk of drug or alcohol use, eating disorder, depression and anxiety, and suicidal thoughts and actions.[38]

The Mayo Clinic identifies four groups of PTSD symptoms:
1. Intrusive Memories
   - Nightmares and/or flashbacks
   - Severe emotional distress or physical reactions when reminded of the event
   - Recurrent and distressing memories of the event
2. Negative changes in thinking and mood
   - Feelings of hopelessness
   - Feeling numb and detached
   - Lack of interest in activities/socialising
   - Withdrawal from friends, family
   - Negative thoughts about self, others or the world
   - Difficulty maintaining close relationships
3. Avoidance
   - Avoid talking and thinking about the event
   - Avoid people, places, activities that remind the person of the event
4. Changes in physical and emotional reactions
   - Easily startled or frightened
   - Always on guard for danger

---

[38] Ibid.

- Sleeping problems
- Difficulty concentrating
- Mood swings
- Feelings of guilt or shame
- Self-destructive behaviours, e.g., drinking too much

Treatment
- Get help! Talk to your doctor.
- Medication: Antianxiety or antidepressant medications may help.
- Counselling: Cognitive Behavioural Therapy (CBT) has been shown to be effective.[39]
- Support groups
- Talk to friends and family, spiritual/religious leader.
- Meditation, relaxation techniques
- Contact the Canadian Mental Health Association (CMHA, www.cmha.ca), or your local mental health agency for supports and resources in your area.
- Please refer to Appendices I, III, and V for additional information.
- If you think you may hurt yourself or plan to commit suicide, call 911 immediately.

---

[39] The Canadian Mental Health Association,
https://cmha.ca/documents/post-traumatic-stress-disorder-ptsd

Bibliography

Amen, Daniel G. (2015). *Change Your Brain, Change Your Life: The Breakthrough Program for Conquering Anxiety, Depression, Obsessiveness, Lack of Focus, Anger, and Memory Problems.* Harmony books, New York: NY

Bialosky, Jill. (2011). *History Of A Suicide: My Sister's Unfinished Life.* Washington Square Press, New York: NY

Dyer, Wayne. W. (2014). *I Can See Clearly Now.* Hay House Inc, USA

Haig, Matt. (2015). *Reasons to Stay Alive.* Harper Collins Publisher Ltd., Toronto: ONT

Hay, Louise. (2004). *You Can Heal Your Life.* Hay House Inc, USA

Hughes, Clara. (2015). *Open Heart, Open Mind.* Simon And Schuster, Toronto: Canada

Kirshenbaum, M. (2004). *Everything Happens for a Reason.* Three Rivers Press (Random House Inc), New York: NY

Lee, R.T. and Brotheridge, C.M. (2006). "When prey turns predatory: Workplace bullying as a predictor of counter aggression/bullying, coping and well being." C.M. *European Journal of Work and Organization Psychology,* **00(0)**: 1-26

Myss, Caroline. (2004). *Invisible Acts of Power: Channeling Grace in Your Everyday Life.* Simon and Schuster Inc., New York: NY

Newman, M., Berkowitz, B., and Owen, J. (1973). *How to Be Your Own Best Friend,* Ballantine Books, New York: NY

Scheff, Sue. (2014). *Adult Bullying.* Retrieved from http://www.huffingtonpost.com

Styron, William. (1992). *Darkness Visible; A Memoir of Madness.* First Vintage Books Ed, New York: NY

Williams, M., Teasdale, J., Segal, Z & Kabat-Zinn, J. (2007). *The Mindful Way through Depression. Freeing Yourself from Chronic Unhappiness.* The Guilford Press, New York: NY

Workplace Bullying Institute. (2017) *Bullying Statistics.* Retrieved from http://www.bullyingstatisitcs.org

Websites

"Getting Back to Happy." www.marcandangel.com

"Sick Not Weak" by Michael Langsberg. https://sicknotweak.com

Book Cover Acknowledgements

Book Cover Design and Interior Illustrations
by Julie Saeger Nierenberg
www.createwriteenterprises.com

Author Photographs
by Julie Pringle, SNAP Photography
www.snapcommercial.ca

Hair
by Dani Mackriss
www.orahspasalon.com

Make up
by Heather Gillett
www.hgmua.com

Tracey Maxfield

Contact Information

You may learn more about Tracey and follow her future contributions at the following Internet sites.

- Website: www.TraceyMaxfield.com
- Facebook: www.facebook.com/Tracey.Maxfield.90
- YouTube: https://youtu.be/GwXrUqEYIos
- Twitter: @TraceyMaxfield
- Instagram: www.instagram.com/TraceyMaxfield/
- Pinterest: www.pinterest.ca/forrestermaxfie/

Made in the USA
San Bernardino, CA
12 October 2018